Jazz Theory Workbook

Jazz Theory Workbook accompanies the second edition of the successful *Jazz Theory—From Basic to Advanced Study* textbook, designed for undergraduate and graduate students studying jazz. The overall pedagogy bridges theory and practice, combining theory, aural skills, keyboard skills, and improvisation into a comprehensive whole. While the Companion Website for the textbook features aural and play-along exercises, along with some written exercises and the answer key, this workbook contains brand-new written exercises, as well as four appendices: (1) Rhythmic Exercises, (2) Common-Practice Harmony at the Keyboard, (3) Jazz Harmony at the Keyboard, and (4) Patterns for Jazz Improvisation. *Jazz Theory Workbook* works in tandem with its associated textbook in the same format as the 27-chapter book, yet is also designed to be used on its own, providing students and readers with quick access to all relevant exercises without the need to download or print pages that inevitably must be written out. The workbook is sold both on its own as well as discounted in a package with the textbook. *Jazz Theory Workbook* particularly serves the ever-increasing population of classical students interested in jazz theory or improvisation.

Dariusz Terefenko is Associate Professor of Jazz and Contemporary Media at the Eastman School of Music, University of Rochester.

Jazz Theory Workbook

From Basic to Advanced Study

Dariusz Terefenko

Routledge
Taylor & Francis Group

NEW YORK AND LONDON

First published 2020
by Routledge
52 Vanderbilt Avenue, New York, NY 10017

and by Routledge
2 Park Square, Milton Park, Abingdon, Oxon, OX14 4RN

Routledge is an imprint of the Taylor & Francis Group, an informa business

Library of Congress Cataloging-in-Publication Data
Names: Terefenko, Dariusz, 1968– author.
Title: Jazz theory workbook : from basic to advanced study /
   Dariusz Terefenko.
Description: New York ; London : Routledge, 2019.
Identifiers: LCCN 2019013750 (print) | LCCN 2019017319 (ebook) |
   ISBN 9780429445477 (ebook) | ISBN 9781138334243 (hardback) |
   ISBN 9781138334250 (pbk.)
Subjects: LCSH: Music theory. | Jazz—Instruction and study.
Classification: LCC MT6 (ebook) | LCC MT6 .T3705 2019 (print) |
   DDC 781.65/12—dc23
LC record available at https://lccn.loc.gov/2019013750

ISBN: 978-1-138-33424-3 (hbk)
ISBN: 978-1-138-33425-0 (pbk)
ISBN: 978-0-429-44547-7 (ebk)

Typeset in Galliard and Swiss 721
by Apex CoVantage LLC

Visit the Companion Website: www.routledge.com/cw/terefenko2e

To my beloved mother

Contents

Preface

In the era of computers, smartphones, iPads, and other electronic gadgets, a return to old-fashioned musical activities such as (1) writing music on paper with a pencil; (2) transcribing solos; (3) performing rhythm with your hands; (4) learning music theory at the keyboard; (5) transposing to all keys; (6) composing on paper; and many others might not be as thrilling as using the latest computer apps or browsing through digital media, but they can still be quite effective as valuable pedagogical strategies. Just as in the past when these types of activities were the norm, they can still prove indispensable to the learning process to internalize and retain theoretical/practical concepts, whether from common-practice or jazz traditions.

This workbook is designed to accompany my *Jazz Theory—From Basic to Advanced Study* (2nd ed., Routledge 2018). The overall organization of the workbook is similar to the textbook: Parts I, II, and III contain 27 chapters (just like the textbook), followed by four free-standing appendices. The workbook contains a number of written and practical assignments that are presented in a pedagogically convincing way, which makes the study of jazz theory more palatable and attractive to various demographics of readers. The material presented in this workbook is just as suitable for college students as it is for music professionals and pedagogues. In fact, the content of the four appendices might appeal even more to the latter demographics of readers, as it features a comprehensive yet condensed overview of four subjects: (1) rhythm; (2) common-practice harmony; (3) jazz harmony; and (4) jazz improvisation. Each subject is presented from a practical perspective devoid of extraneous theoretical explanations and covers a broad spectrum of interrelated topics.

Each chapter in the first part of the workbook has two or three sections. In Chapters 1–10, the first section is entitled "Master the Fundamentals"; in Chapters 11–19, "Fundamentals to Mastery"; and in Chapters 20–27, "Mastery to Excellence." These sections contain a selection of comprehensive questions and topics for discussion that thoroughly cover the material from the corresponding chapters in the textbook. The second and third sections are entitled "Test Your Knowledge," "Explore the Possibilities," "Play and Sing," "Musical Analysis," "Transcription," or "Test Your Knowledge" and are more practical, with a series of written exercises, analytical assignments, composition tasks, and others. Together with the first section, they offer valuable pedagogical resources to fully internalize the content of each chapter. Unlike the first half of the workbook, which neatly parallels the content of the textbook, the appendices contain more comprehensive material, which takes much longer to study and could not be presented in a pedagogically sound manner within the boundaries of the textbook chapters. Such organization allows the reader to work on the content of individual appendices independently from the textbook. The compilation of all necessary resources on rhythm, common-practice harmony, jazz harmony, and jazz improvisation within individual appendices allows the reader easy access, which in turn expedites the learning process and eliminates the need to look for snippets of that material elsewhere. For instance, the concept of voice leading is discussed throughout the textbook with few practical illustrations demonstrating its fundamental claims. In the workbook, on the other hand, that concept is shown in the form of various chord progressions with (1) different harmonic settings; (2) different tonal/functional contexts; (3) keyboard and chorale textures; and (4) necessary exceptions to the voice-leading norms, so that the reader can experience that concept more fully.

Appendix A, "Rhythmic Exercises," contains 180 exercises to be performed with a metronome. Just as with the content of other appendices, the exercises in Appendix A are organized progressively from simple to difficult (with tripartite division into "Master the Fundamentals," "Fundamentals to Mastery," and "Mastery to Excellence" sections). Each exercise has a range of specified tempi at which that exercise should be performed (either by tapping your hands or playing on an instrument: i.e. single or two notes). It is advisable to start each exercise at a comfortable tempo and gradually increase the speed until the maximum tempo is reached. Since the majority of exercises are rather short, it is suggested to loop each exercise to the point of performing it comfortably with all performance-related details (articulation, accents, feel, etc.) and eventually memorizing it. Notice that there are no written instructions regarding the interpretation of swing as opposed to straight 8th notes, nor are there guidelines explaining how to play on "two and four" as opposed to "one and three." These guidelines can be easily found in the textbook, as specified by the corresponding endnotes. Since rhythm is considered to be one of the most important components in jazz (see Chapter 2 in the textbook), it is essential to master it and explore its vast possibilities. Once the reader reaches Unit 6 ("4/4 Meter—Swing Rhythms") and Unit 7 ("3/4 Meter—Swing Rhythms"), the study of jazz rhythm commences in earnest as each eight-bar phrase features an idiomatic rhythmic design, which can be added to your rhythmic vocabulary and eventually implemented in jazz improvisation. It cannot be stressed enough the importance of practicing rhythm with a metronome and employing minute tempo variations as you tap or play the rhythms on your instrument.

At first glance, the content of Appendix B, "Common-Practice Harmony at the Keyboard," might raise some eyebrows from jazz purists given that the workbook is supposed to be a compendium for a jazz theory textbook. I strongly believe that the knowledge of common-practice harmony not only goes hand in hand with jazz harmony but also constitutes a prerequisite stepping stone for further exploration of the jazz harmonic syntax. In addition, common-practice harmony offers many valuable lessons that contemporary jazz musicians can take advantage of. Indeed, while the idea of interdisciplinary crossovers between common-practice and jazz traditions is one of the leading leitmotifs unfolding in the textbook, it is in the workbook that it becomes manifest even more strongly. Appendix B, then, has two major objectives: (1) it prepares the reader for the content of Appendix C, "Jazz Harmony at the Keyboard," and (2) it offers a complete overview of essential topics in common-practice harmony conveniently compiled in one place. The latter objective might prove quite valuable to music pedagogues searching for new harmonic drills to complement their teaching.

It was actually a student at the Eastman School of Music who encouraged me to compile the materials for Appendix B. That student was interested in applying for the Advanced Certificate in the Art of Improvisation and inquired about materials to prepare for the keyboard exam. I suggested a number of fine books and quickly realized that while very instructive, none of them included material that was easily perusable and diverse enough that someone with an adequate knowledge of music theory (as my student was) could quickly access and use to get ready for the exam. I hope that Appendix B fills that void and offers a useful compendium of practical resources for students, teachers, and those who want to hone their keyboard skills. Appendix B has 22 units, with such diverse topics as (1) lead-sheet, Roman numerals, and figured-bass realization; (2) cadential gestures; (3) partimenti (selected from the many available collections by Handel, Tritto, Fenaroli, Sala, Paisiello, Durante, Pasquini, Pogliettis, Furno, and others); (4) galant schematas (courtesy of Robert Gjergingen's seminal treatise); (5) historical evolution of the Rule of the Octave; (6) chromaticism; (7) keyboard and chorale realization; (8) melody harmonization; (9) stylized harmony; and others. By carefully studying each unit, the reader will learn about (1) the rules of voice leading; (2) the dissonance treatment; (3) the functional distribution of chords in harmonic progression; (4) the tonal potential of advanced harmonic formations; and (5) harmonic trademarks of Richard Wagner, Gabriel Fauré, Claude Debussy, Alexander Scriabin, Max Reger, and Olivier Messiaen, among many other topics. As you will notice, the emphasis is on (1) playing in keyboard and/or chorale texture (thoroughly explained in *Jazz Theory—From Basic to Advanced Study*); (2) transposition to different keys; and (3) music analysis.

Topics presented in Appendix B (as well as in other appendices) are devoid of extensive theoretical discussions. I quickly realized that by adding even a couple of paragraphs on each topic, the length of the appendix would greatly exceed the length of the entire workbook, which might be problematic for the publisher. If some of the topics seem unfamiliar to the reader, they can be easily found elsewhere, as indicated by the endnotes. Remember that the objectives of Appendix B are (1) to develop functional keyboard skills; (2) to offer a brief synopsis of various harmonic topics; and (3) to foster muscle memory in the fingers. When theoretical curiosity arises, one can easily fulfill that desire by consulting many reliable sources. Just as is the case with rhythmic drills in Appendix A, each harmonic exercise in Appendix B (364 in total) should be played from beginning to end without stopping and at a comfortable tempo. Even though the guidelines for each exercise specify playing in additional keys, for best results, perform all exercises in all keys.

In a way, Appendix C, "Jazz Harmony at the Keyboard," is a continuation of Appendix B. In fact, the final unit of Appendix B—"Stylized Harmony"—includes a number of keyboard drills analyzed with jazz chord symbols, which demonstrate just how inventive and powerful the harmonic languages of various composers truly are and how they can be rediscovered by jazz musicians. With a total of 12 units and 281 exercises, Appendix C complements the content of *Jazz Theory—From Basic to Advanced Study* in a fairly logical way. For instance, the keyboard drills from Unit 1 ("Four-Part Chords"), Unit 2 ("Five-Part Chords"), and Unit 3 ("Six-Part Chords") offer an exhaustive supplement to the content of Chapters 4, 5, and 11 in the textbook. These drills serve purely utilitarian objectives: they familiarize the reader with a multitude of harmonic choices and prepare for every conceivable scenario one might encounter while realizing harmonic progressions. Just as in Appendix B, the emphasis is on playing in various keyboard and chorale textures, and on transposition to all keys. The additional objective of Appendix C—maybe even a fundamental one—is to develop a set of functional keyboard skills that would allow the reader to comfortably realize any jazz progression.

The ability to play a keyboard instrument in a functional way (i.e. accompanying instrumentalists/vocalist or playing with a rhythm section) is an indispensable skill that every musician should possess. The content of Units 9 through 12 is specifically designed to achieve that important objective. The exercises presented in these units are written with the intent of being playable by everyone regardless of one's keyboard proficiency. For instance, various blues progressions (discussed in Chapters 9 and 15 in the textbook) are realized with (1) a simple keyboard texture; (2) a more advanced walking bass texture; and (3) stylized stride accompaniments. Similarly, the chord progression from the A section of "Take the A Train" receives half a dozen stylistic treatments, as do various two- and four-bar turnaround progressions. It is recommended these exercises be performed with a metronome and in transposition to all keys. As you familiarize yourself with different methods of keyboard and chorale style playing, try experimenting with these stylistic paradigms with chord progressions from different standard tunes and jazz instrumentals.

Appendix D, "Patterns for Jazz Improvisation," is organized in a fairly straightforward manner. It includes eight units with 135 ideas for jazz improvisation. These ideas are in the form of 4-bar patterns, 8-bar phrases, complete choruses, and rhythmic solos to be melodically realized. For instance, Units 1 and 2 contain a total of 75 patterns for major and minor versions of the II—V—I progression, and Units 4 through 6 demonstrate various approaches to practicing jazz improvisation based on different blues progressions (basic blues, minor blues, "Billie's Bounce," "Blues for Alice," and the "Dance of the Infidels") and "Confirmation" and rhythm changes. The majority of the melodic ideas in Appendix D can be practiced with audio clips (recorded by the author with a live rhythm section); these can be found at www.routledge.com/cw/terefenko2e and www.routledgetextbooks.com/textbooks/9780415537612/AppendixC.pdf—*Play Along Sessions*, Tracks: 1–35.

In conclusion, this workbook for *Jazz Theory—From Basic to Advanced Study* (2nd ed., Routledge 2018) offers a broad spectrum of written assignments, practical drills, and didactic materials that can be used in tandem with my textbook or separately by someone with ample knowledge of music theory. The overall design—27 chapters and four independent appendices—makes it attractive to four types of musicians: (1) jazz aficionados; (2) classical musicians willing to sharpen their practical skills; (3) jazz and classical college students; and (4) professors searching for new teaching resources. It is my hope that this workbook fulfills the stated objectives and provides a wealth of pedagogical resources for years to come.

Basics

PART ONE

CHAPTER 1

Music Fundamentals

MASTER THE FUNDAMENTALS

1. Explain the difference between octave equivalence and enharmonic equivalence.

2. List all major sharp keys with their relative partners in the order they appear in the circle of fifths.

3. List all major flat keys with their relative partners in the order they appear in the circle of fifths.

4. Provide a definition of musical meter. What rhythmic elements are necessary to establish a musical meter?

5. Discuss the different types of meter occurring in music.

6. What is the difference between the downbeat and the upbeat?

7. How many semitones does the major scale have? Where do they occur in the scale?

8. How many semitones does the minor scale have (natural, harmonic, and melodic), and between which scale degrees do they occur?

9. Describe different methods of labeling intervals.

10. Name all diatonic and chromatic intervals within the octave.

11. How many semitones does each interval within the octave have?

12. Explain the difference between:

    a. Melodic and harmonic intervals

    b. Diatonic and chromatic intervals

    c. Simple and compound intervals

13. Describe the pitch and intervallic content of four basic triadic formations.

14. Name the lowest pitch of the following triads:

    a. Am in second inversion

    b. EM in first inversion

    c. Fdim in second inversion

    d.   B♭m in first inversion

    e.   A♭aug in second inversion

    f.   C♯sus in first inversion

    g.   GM in second inversion

15. Discuss the unique characteristics of the augmented triad.

16. How is the suspended triad different from other types of triadic formations?

TEST YOUR KNOWLEDGE

1. Write the following pitches in the score.

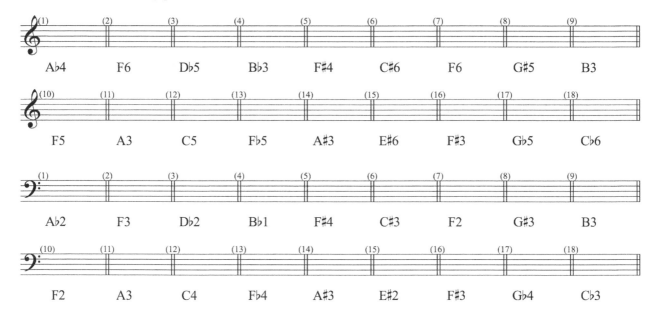

2. Label each note on the staff with two different letter names along with their octave designation.

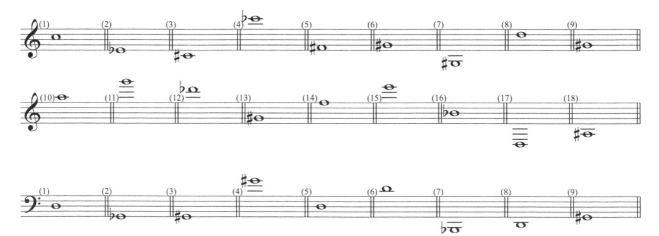

3. Write the following scales using accidentals.

(1) B♭ major ascending

(2) F♯ major ascending

(3) G major descending

(4) B major descending

(5) D harmonic minor ascending

(6) G♯ melodic minor descending

(7) B harmonic minor descending

(8) E♭ major ascending

(9) E melodic minor descending

(10) A♭ major ascending

4. Write the following scales using key signatures.

(1) B♭ harmonic minor ascending

(2) F♯ melodic minor descending

(3) D major descending

(4) C♯ major descending

(5) B harmonic minor ascending

(6) D♯ melodic minor ascending

(7) F harmonic minor descending

(8) D♭ major ascending

(9) G melodic minor descending

(10) B major ascending

5.   Identify the following major keys.

6.   Identify the following minor keys.

7.   Identify the following melodic and harmonic intervals.

8.   Realize the following chord symbols on the staff below.

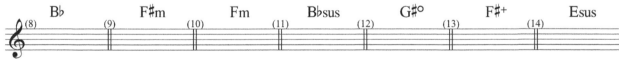

CHAPTER 2

Jazz Rhythms

MASTER THE FUNDAMENTALS

1. What is swing? Provide two alternative definitions.

2. What musical elements are necessary to convey a "swing feel"?

3. Discuss the role of rhythm in jazz.

4. What are the main differences between rhythm in jazz and rhythm in common-practice music?

5. Name at least three idiomatic rhythmic and metric events that occur in jazz and explain their *modus operandi*.

6. What is the relationship between written "swing 8ths" and their musical interpretation?

7. On your instrument, demonstrate the different kinds of swing 8th notes.

8. What is the relationship between the tempo of musical performance and the location of swing 8ths within the beat and measure?

9. Compare the distribution of metrical accents in jazz as opposed to music from South America.

10. Describe the rhythmic organization of music from three different South American countries.

11. Provide a definition for the following terms associated with South American music:

    a. Samba

    b. Clave

    c. Partido alto

    d. Cáscara

    e. Bossa nova

TEST YOUR KNOWLEDGE

1.   Using the rule of "visible beat 3," rewrite the incorrectly notated rhythms on the lower staff.

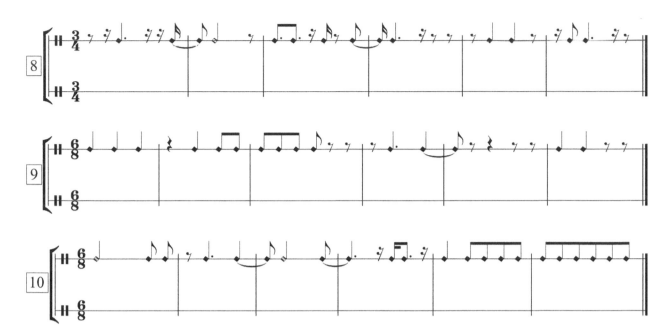

2. Based on the specified meter, group the following unmeasured rhythmic values in complete measures.

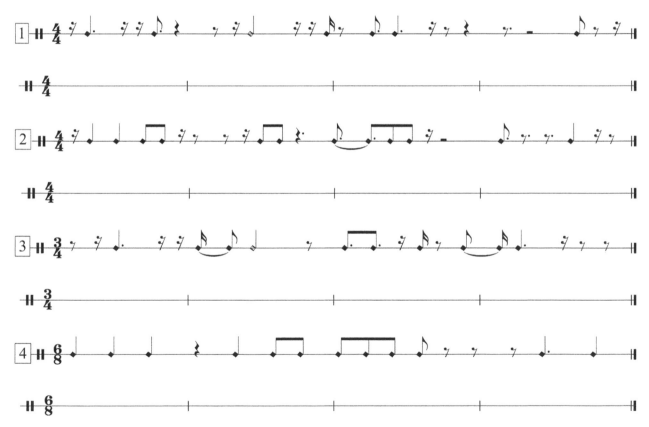

CHAPTER 3

Harmonic Function

MASTER THE FUNDAMENTALS

1. What is functional tonality?

2. What types of tonal functions exist in common-practice music? What are their main characteristics?

3. Provide the name for each scale degree in major and minor keys.

4. Explain the difference between primary and secondary chords.

5. Assign functional status to secondary triads in major.

6. Establish a network of functional relationships between primary and secondary triads in major.

7. Assign functional status to secondary triads in minor.

8. Establish a network of functional relationships between primary and secondary triads in minor.

9. Discuss the strengths and weaknesses of lead-sheet notation.

10. Discuss the strengths and weaknesses of Roman numeral notation.

11. Discuss the strengths and weaknesses of functional notation.

12. What is the difference between musical events occurring at the structural versus surface level? Provide an example.

13. What is a pivot chord?

14. What role does a pivot chord play in harmonic progressions? Provide an example.

15. What is a cadence?

16. What types of cadential formulas occur in common-practice music?

17. Describe the unfolding of harmonic function in five different cadential formulas.

18. What kind of musical event is a prolongation? Provide an example.

19. In what ways does musical context determine a chord's function?

20. What are the most fundamental rules of voice leading?

21. Explain the main differences between the rules of voice leading in jazz versus common-practice music.

22. Draw parallels between voice leading in jazz and common-practice music.

23. What types of melodic motions occur in music? Describe their main attributes.

24. What type of melodic motion is the most desirable in harmonic progressions and why?

25. What are the main characteristics of keyboard style texture?

26. What are the main characteristics of chorale style texture?

27. Demonstrate the "rule of the nearest way" when connecting chords related by (1) descending/ascending fifths; (2) descending/ascending seconds; and (3) descending/ascending thirds.

28. Provide a definition of outer-voice counterpoint. What is its role while realizing harmonic progressions?

TEST YOUR KNOWLEDGE

1. Using lead-sheet notation, label the following triads.

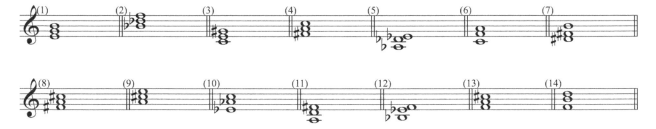

2. Using the "rule of the nearest way," realize the following progressions in keyboard style.

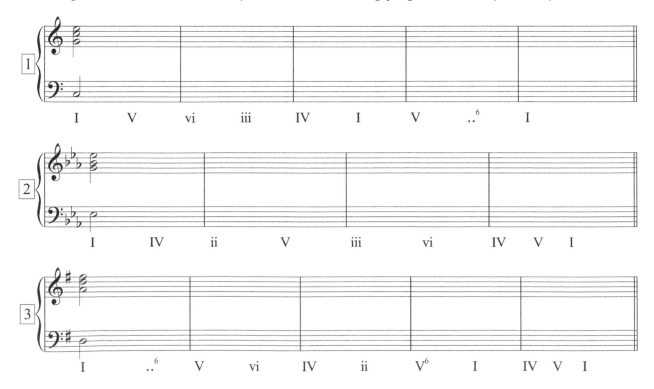

MUSICAL ANALYSIS

3. Analyze the following chord progressions using (1) Roman numerals, (2) lead-sheet notation, (3) functional symbols, and (4) scale degrees for the soprano voice.

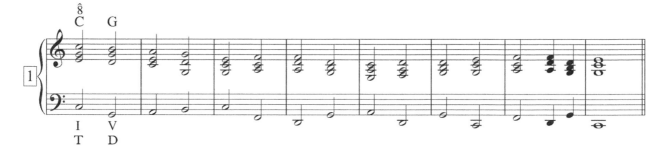

Four-Part Chords

MASTER THE FUNDAMENTALS

1. How does the harmonic syntax in jazz differ from that of common-practice music?

2. Explain the status of a major 6th and a major 7th within the chord's structure.

3. List all four-part chords belonging to the major category of chords. Describe their pitch content, functional tendencies, and practical applications.

4. List all four-part chords belonging to the minor category of chords. Describe their pitch content, functional tendencies, and practical applications.

5. List all four-part chords belonging to the dominant category of chords. Describe their pitch content, functional tendencies, and practical applications.

6. List all four-part chords belonging to the intermediary category of chords. Describe their pitch content, functional tendencies, and practical applications.

7. What is the difference between the regular dominant 7th and the suspended dominant 7th?

8. Which notes within a chord are referred to as the essential chord tones?

9. What is the difference between the m7(♭5) and ø7 chord? Explain each chord's functional behavior and specify a context in which they are likely to occur. Provide an example.

10. Discuss the strengths and weaknesses of figured-bass notation.

11. Explain the notation of non-harmonic tones using figured-bass symbols.

12. Provide figured-bass symbols for the following four-part chords in:

    a. Root position

    b. First inversion

    c. Second inversion

    d. Third inversion

13. Discuss the potential of inversional equivalence of chords in jazz harmony.

14. What does the term "voicing" refer to?

15. What is the difference between open and close voicings?

16. Describe the process of generating "drop 2" voicings. Provide an example.

17. Which member of a chord determines its position?

18. How many positions does any four-part chord have?

TEST YOUR KNOWLEDGE

1. Notate the following four-part chords in close position.

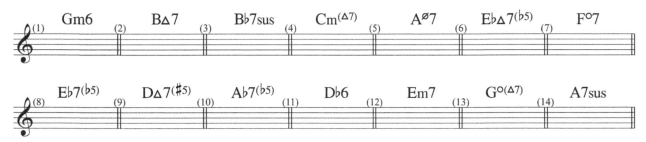

2. Provide lead-sheet symbols for the following four-part chords.

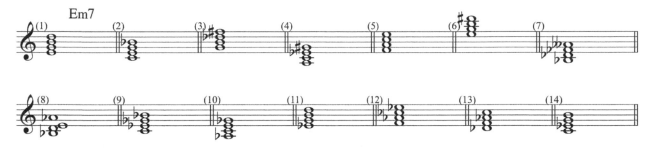

3. Analyze the following chords using figured-bass notation.

4. Using the setting of DM7 as a model, realize the following four-part chords as "drop 2" voicings.

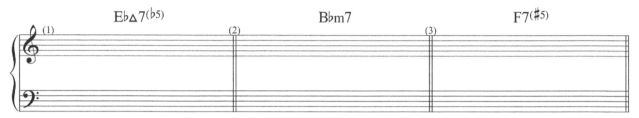

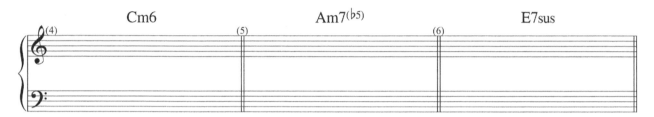

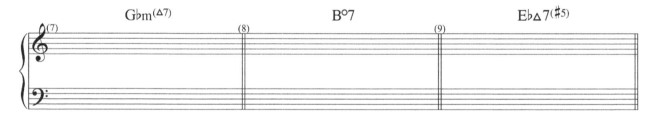

PLAY AND SING

5. While playing the content of the two bottom staves on a keyboard, sing the assigned chord members.

CHAPTER 5

Five-Part Chords

MASTER THE FUNDAMENTALS

1. Which chord members are known as chordal extensions?

2. Explain the difference between an essential chord tone and a chordal extension.

3. Discuss the relationship between chordal extensions and harmonic partials in the overtone series.

4. What types of chordal extensions are admissible in the context of:

    a.   Major chords

    b.   Minor chords

    c.   Dominant chords

    d.   Dominant suspended chords

    e.   Diminished chords

    f.   Half-diminished chords

5. Explain the difference between a 6th functioning as the essential chord member and a 13th functioning as the chordal extension.

6. Discuss the impact of diatonic versus chromatic extensions on the overall sound of harmonic formations. Provide an example.

7. What specific issues are involved in the concept of "dissonance treatment"?

8. Explain the difference between a pitch alteration and a chordal extension.

9. List all five-part chords belonging to the major category. Describe their pitch content, functional behaviors, and practical applications.

10. List all five-part chords belonging to the minor category. Describe their pitch content, functional behaviors, and practical applications.

11. List all five-part chords belonging to the dominant category. Describe their pitch content, functional behaviors, and practical applications.

12. List all five-part chords belonging to the suspended dominant category. Describe their pitch content, functional behaviors, and practical applications.

13. List all five-part chords belonging to the intermediary category. Describe their pitch content, functional behaviors, and practical applications.

14. Explain the process of generating "drop 2" five-part voicings.

15. What is the intervallic content of the L.H. in a "drop 2" (1) first position voicing; (2) second position voicing; (3) third position voicing; and (4) fourth position voicing?

TEST YOUR KNOWLEDGE

1. Notate the following five-part chords in close position.

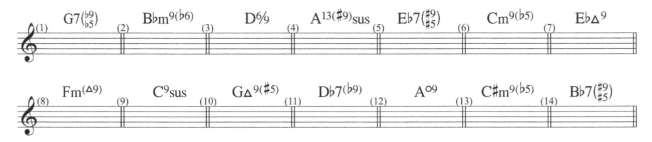

2. Provide lead-sheet symbols for the following five-part chords.

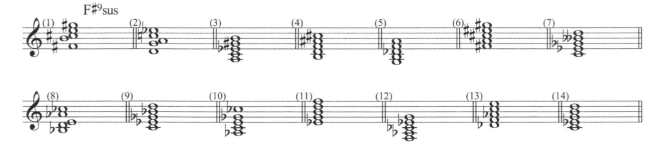

3. Using the setting of F#9sus as a model, realize the following five-part chords as "drop 2" voicings.

PLAY AND SING

4. While playing the content of the bottom two staves on a keyboard, sing the assigned chord members.

CHAPTER 6
The II—V—I Progression

MASTER THE FUNDAMENTALS

1. Discuss the historical evolution of the II—V—I progression in jazz.

2. Describe the use of a ii—V^7—I progression in three different jazz styles.

3. Explain the role of different kinds of diminished 7th chord in chord progressions.

4. What is the harmonic potential of a common-tone diminished 7th chord? What stylistic effect does it generate? Provide an example.

5. What is the relationship between a common-tone diminished 7th chord and the blues?

6. Discuss the role of passing diminished 7th chord in jazz harmony. Provide an example.

7. What is the potential of a neighbor diminished 7th chord in jazz harmony? Provide an example.

8. Map each chord from the II—V—I progression onto a specific harmonic function.

9. Provide a definition of guide tones. Discuss their roles in jazz harmony and improvisation.

10. Discuss the use of secondary dominants in jazz harmony. Provide an example.

11. Provide a definition of invertible counterpoint at the octave.

12. Explore the potential of invertible counterpoint at the octave in jazz harmony and improvisation.

13. Explain the process of transforming a diminished 7th chord into a [ii—V^7]/V progression. Provide an example.

14. Discuss the process of tonicization and its role in jazz harmony. Provide an example.

15. What is a harmonic elision? Provide an example.

TEST YOUR KNOWLEDGE

1. Using the guide tones of underlying chords, realize the following progressions.

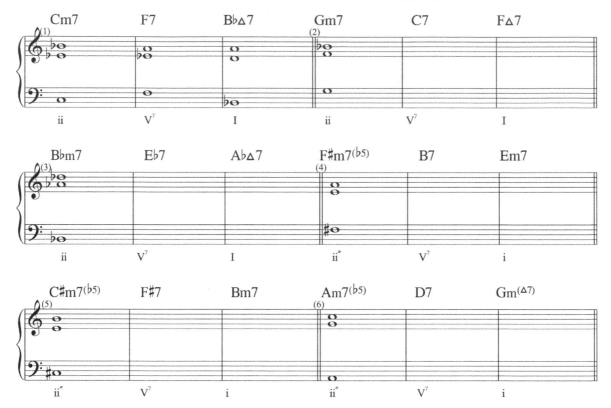

2. Realize the II—V—I progressions using "drop 2" four-part voicings. Maintain a good voice leading. The opening chord is provided.

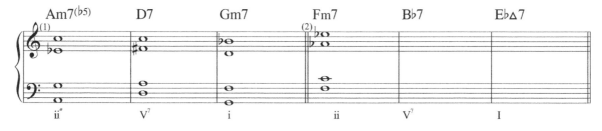

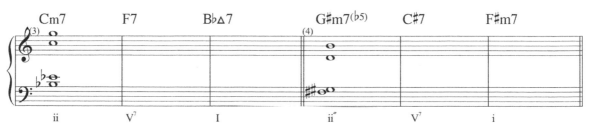

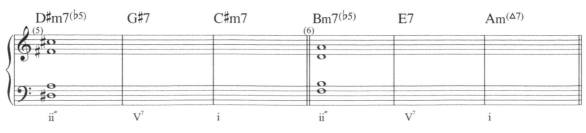

3. Realize the II—V—I progressions using "drop 2" five-part voicings. Maintain a good voice leading. The opening chord is provided.

4. Each progression contains different kinds of diminished 7th chords. Locate and label them, analyze their functional behavior, and develop a contextual analysis using Roman numerals and lead-sheet symbols. The first progression is fully realized.

PLAY AND SING

5. While playing the content of the bottom two staves on a keyboard, sing the assigned chord members.

CHAPTER 7
Modes

MASTER THE FUNDAMENTALS

1. Explain the role of beauty marks in modal scales.

2. What is the difference between avoid notes and beauty marks?

3. Which notes within a mode are essential to convey its modal attributes?

4. What is the difference between the Phrygian and Locrian mode?

5. What is the difference between the Dorian and Aeolian mode?

6. How many beauty marks does the Altered mode have?

7. What is the difference between the Lydian augmented and Mixolydian #11 mode?

8. List all the modes that belong to the major category. Describe their pitch structures and discuss their potential for jazz improvisation.

9. List all the modes that belong to the minor category. Describe their pitch structures and discuss their potential for jazz improvisation.

10. Explain the role of chromaticism in jazz harmony and improvisation.

TEST YOUR KNOWLEDGE

1. Notate the following diatonic modes on the staff. Analyze their pitch content in terms of essential chord members, beauty marks, and chordal extensions.

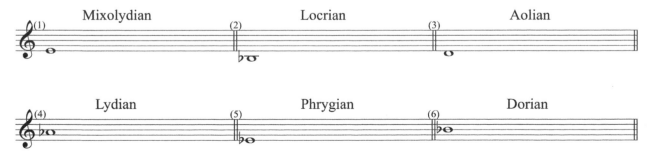

2. Notate the following chromatic modes on the staff. Analyze their pitch content in terms of essential chord members, beauty marks, and chordal extensions.

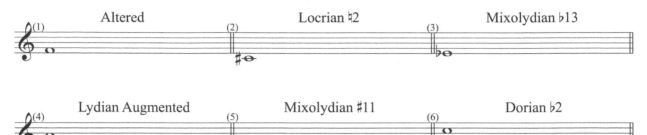

3. Identify the following diatonic modes. Analyze their pitch content in terms of essential chord members, beauty marks, and chordal extensions.

4. Identify the following diatonic modes. Analyze their pitch content in terms of essential chord members, beauty marks, and chordal extensions.

EXPLORE THE POSSIBILITIES

5. Compose a 16-bar jazz phrase using the following modes. Be able to play them on your instrument.

   a. C Aeolian

   b. A♭ Lydian

   c. B Lydian Augmented

   d. G Melodic Minor

   e. F Locrian

   f. C♯ Dorian

   g. D♭ Altered

   h. E Mixolydian ♯11

   i. B♭ Mixolydian ♭13

   j. A♭ Mixolydian

   k. A Dorian ♭2

   l. D Locrian ♮2

   m. E♭ Ionian

   n. F Phrygian

CHAPTER 8

Chord–Scale Theory

MASTER THE FUNDAMENTALS

1. Discuss the main claims of chord–scale theory.

2. Compare and contrast the use of Dorian functioning as a minor tonic as opposed to a predominant mode. Provide an example.

3. List all the modes belonging to the major category; specify their functional behaviors and establish a chord–scale relationship for each mode.

4. Discuss ways in which quartal structures can effectively be utilized in jazz harmony. Provide an example.

5. List all the modes belonging to the minor category; specify their functional behaviors and establish a chord–scale relationship for each mode.

6. Select a characteristic upper-structure triad that best captures the sound of each diatonic and chromatic mode. Analyze its pitch content in relation to the corresponding mode.

7. List all the modes belonging to the dominant category; specify their functional behaviors and establish a chord–scale relationship for each mode.

8. How are gapped formations different from other types of voicings?

9. List all the modes belonging to the suspended dominant category; specify their functional behaviors and establish a chord–scale relationship for each mode.

10. Explain the mutual relationship between melodic and harmonic dimensions in music.

11. List all the modes belonging to the intermediary category; specify their functional behaviors and establish a chord–scale relationship for each mode.

12. Provide two alternate chord–scale relationships for a ii—V^7—I progression.

13. Provide two alternate chord–scale relationships for a ii$^\emptyset$—V^7—i progression.

TEST YOUR KNOWLEDGE

1. For each of the following chords, establish a convincing chord–scale relationship.

2. For each of the following scales, establish a convincing chord–scale relationship.

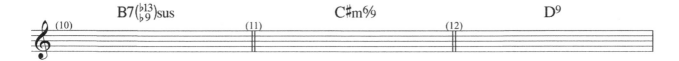

3. For each of the following progressions, establish a convincing chord–scale relationship and notate the correct modes on the staff.

EXPLORE THE POSSIBILITIES

4. Compose a modal piece according to the following formal guidelines:

   A (mm. 1–8)—C Lydian

   B (mm. 9–16)—A♭ Mixolydian

   C (mm. 17–24)—B♭ Lydian Augmented

   D (mm. 25–32)—D Dorian ♭2

   E (mm. 33–40)—G Altered

CHAPTER 9

The Blues

MASTER THE FUNDAMENTALS

1. Describe the formal structure and harmonic properties of the basic blues.

2. Compare and contrast the role of structural versus embellishing chords in the blues.

3. How can the call and response technique be effectively utilized in jazz improvisation?

4. What is the role of blue notes in jazz improvisation?

5. Explain the difference between major and minor blues scales.

6. How is the harmonic framework of generic blues different from the basic blues progression?

7. What harmonic events are likely to occur in m. 8 of the basic blues progression?

8. Explore the potential of blues narration (with its idiomatic AA'B phrase structure) in jazz improvisation.

9. Describe the voice leading between the guide tones in chords related by descending fifths. Provide an example.

10. Describe the voice leading between the guide tones in chords related by descending fourths. Provide an example.

11. What is a tonicization? Provide an example.

12. Discuss the relationship between the basic and minor blues progression.

TEST YOUR KNOWLEDGE

1.   Notate the guide tones for the following blues progressions.

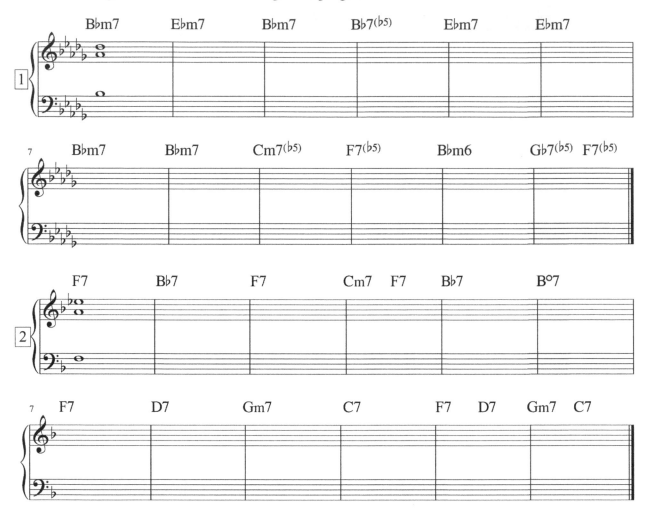

2.   Realize the following blues progressions using "drop 2" five-part voicings.

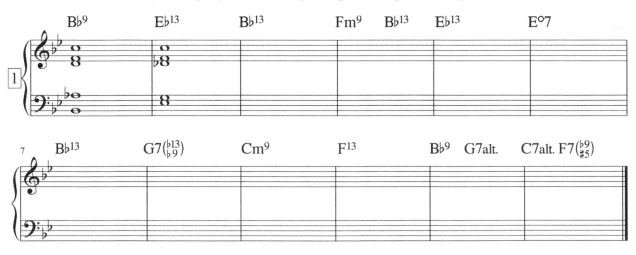

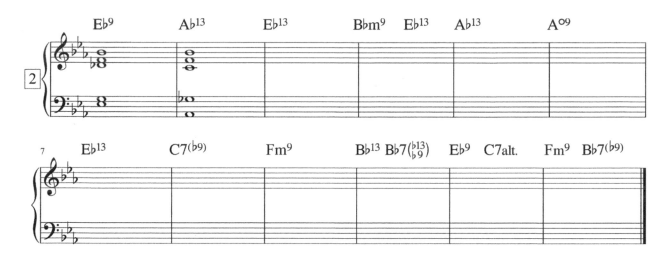

3. Select and notate the appropriate blues scales for the following blues progressions.

4. Select and notate the appropriate modal scales for the following blues progressions.

EXPLORE THE POSSIBILITIES

5. Compose a B♭ blues using the call and response technique with the melodic material drawn entirely from the B♭ minor blues scale.

CHAPTER 10

Basic Improvisation

MASTER THE FUNDAMENTALS

1. Examine the role of rhythm and articulation in jazz improvisation.

2. Discuss challenges that a beginner improviser must overcome while learning how to improvise.

3. Compare and contrast three different styles of jazz improvisation.

4. How does music theory and ear training help in learning jazz improvisation?

5. Provide a definition of blues riffs and examine their potential in jazz improvisation.

6. Discuss the role of guide-tone lines in jazz improvisation.

7. Define a compound melody and explore its potential in jazz improvisation.

8. Describe the rhythmic properties of the Charleston figure. What impact does this figure have on improvisation and comping?

9. What types of techniques of motivic development are often employed in jazz improvisation? Select four techniques and describe their *modus operandi*. Provide an example from the jazz literature.

10. Explain the difference between real and tonal inversion.

EXPLORE THE POSSIBILITIES

1. Compose a 2-chorus blues solo in the key of F major using blues riffs only.

2. Compose a 2-chorus blues solo in the key of G minor using blues riffs only.

Intermediate

CHAPTER 11

Voicing Formations

FUNDAMENTALS TO MASTERY

1. What are the strengths and weaknesses of slash notation? What types of chords are best represented by this notational convention?

2. Explain the role of upper-structure triads within larger harmonic units.

3. Define a polychord. How can it be utilized in jazz harmony? Provide an example.

4. Which major/minor upper-structure triads can be superimposed over major-type chords? Select two polychords and establish a convincing chord–scale relationship for these extended harmonies.

5. Which major/minor upper-structure triads can be superimposed over minor-type chords? Select two polychords and establish a convincing chord–scale relationship for these extended harmonies.

6. Which major/minor upper-structure triads can be superimposed over dominant-type chords? Select two polychords and establish a convincing chord–scale relationship for these extended harmonies.

7. Describe the procedures of generating incomplete voicing formations.

8. Explore the potential of rootless formations in jazz harmony. Provide an example.

9. Discuss the role of rootless formations as effective comping devices.

10. How can tonal and functional ambiguity of rootless formations become a useful asset for jazz musicians to explore?

TEST YOUR KNOWLEDGE

1. Using upper-structure triads, notate the following six-part chords.

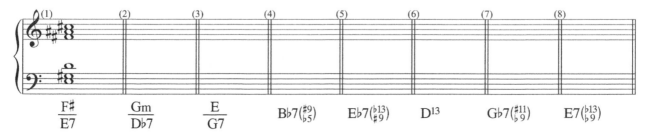

2. Using lead-sheet and slash notation, identify the following chords.

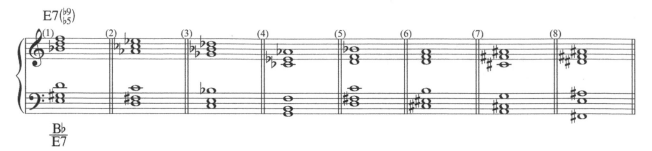

3. Provide a harmonic realization for the following two-note melodic patterns. In your realization, use six-part chords with superimposed upper-structure triads.

EXPLORE THE POSSIBILITIES

4. Using answers provided in m. 1, analyze the following trichords in the context of complete four-, five-, and six-part chords. Enharmonic pitch equivalence is assumed.

5. Using answers provided in m. 1, analyze the following four-part chords in the context of complete four-, five-, and six-part chords. Enharmonic pitch equivalence is assumed.

CHAPTER 12

Keyboard and Jazz Chorale Textures

FUNDAMENTALS TO MASTERY

1. Compare and contrast the realization of a chord progression in keyboard versus chorale style texture.

2. Discuss the role of walking bass in jazz.

3. What are the essential characteristics and stylistic elements of a good walking bass line?

4. Describe each model of keyboard playing and assess its strengths and weaknesses.

5. Which models of keyboard playing are fully functional? In what way are they functional?

6. Which models of keyboard playing are more preparatory in nature? What is their pedagogical role?

7. What types of chordal formations are often employed in chorale style texture?

8. What types of chordal formations are often employed in keyboard style texture?

9. How does the ability to perform all positions of "drop 2" voicings facilitate and improve the realization of harmonic progressions?

10. Examine the potential of invertible counterpoint at the octave in harmonic progressions. Provide an example.

TEST YOUR KNOWLEDGE

1. Using Model I of keyboard playing, realize the following progression.

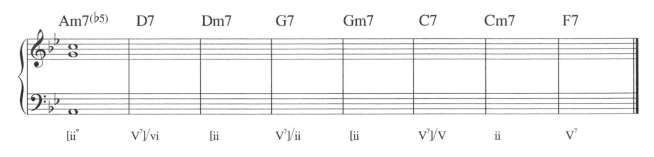

Am7$^{(♭5)}$	D7	Dm7	G7	Gm7	C7	Cm7	F7
[ii°	V^7]/vi	[ii	V^7]/ii	[ii	V^7]/V	ii	V^7

2.   Using Model II of keyboard playing, realize the following progression.

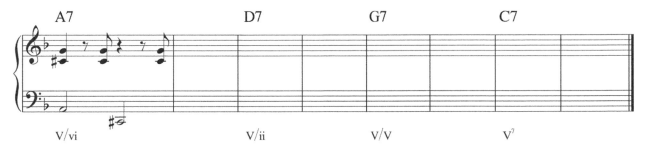

A7	D7	G7	C7
V/vi	V/ii	V/V	V^7

3.   Using Model III of keyboard playing, realize the following progression.

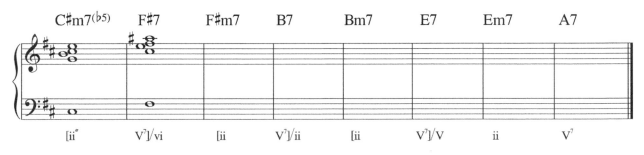

C♯m7$^{(♭5)}$	F♯7	F♯m7	B7	Bm7	E7	Em7	A7
[ii°	V^7]/vi	[ii	V^7]/ii	[ii	V^7]/V	ii	V^7

4.   Using Model IV of keyboard playing, realize the following progression.

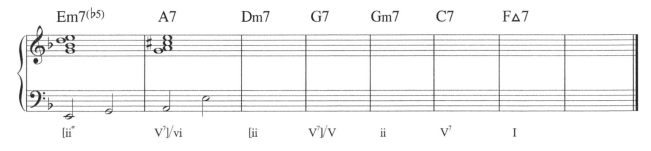

Em7$^{(♭5)}$	A7	Dm7	G7	Gm7	C7	F△7
[ii°	V^7]/vi	[ii	V^7]/V	ii	V^7	I

5.   Using Model V of keyboard playing, realize the following progression.

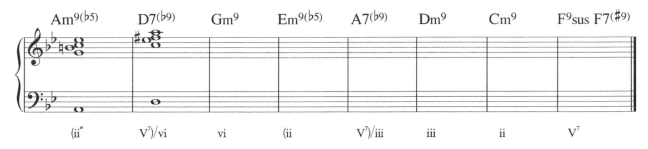

Am$^{9(♭5)}$	D7$^{(♭9)}$	Gm^9	Em$^{9(♭5)}$	A7$^{(♭9)}$	Dm^9	Cm^9	F^{9}sus F7$^{(♯9)}$
(ii°	V^7)/vi	vi	(ii	V^7)/iii	iii	ii	V^7

6. Using Model VI of keyboard playing, realize the following progression.

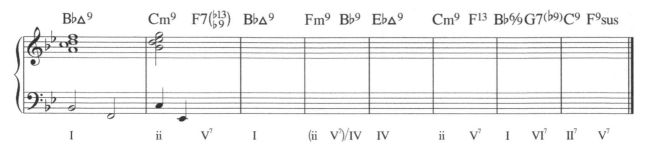

7. Using five-part chorale style texture, realize the following progressions. Analyze each progression with Roman numerals.

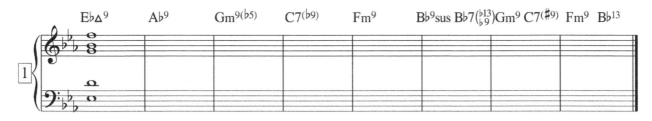

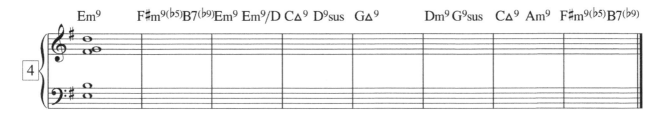

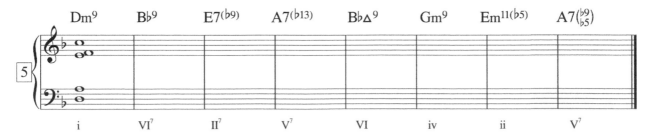

CHAPTER 13

Idiomatic Jazz Progressions

FUNDAMENTALS TO MASTERY

1. Explain the role of tritone substitutions in jazz harmony.

2. Discuss the significance of inversional invariance of the tritone and its impact on the structure of chords, their function, and practical use.

3. What is the role of turnaround progressions in jazz improvisation?

4. What is the effect of applying tritone substitutions to every other chord in the bridge of "I Got Rhythm"?

5. Examine the harmonic structure of the "Lady Bird" turnaround and discuss its relationship to the diatonic I—vi—ii—V^7.

6. What types of harmonic progressions are referred to as "cyclic"?

7. Describe the procedures of generating *Coltrane* substitutions.

8. Compare and contrast the harmonic makeup of *Giant Steps* versus *Countdown* progression.

9. Which diatonic progressions lend themselves for harmonic transformations using *Coltrane* substitutions? Provide an example.

10. Define the musical process known as a modulation. Provide an example.

11. Explain the difference between a modulation and a tonicization.

TEST YOUR KNOWLEDGE

1. Analyze the following chord progressions with Roman numerals and lead-sheet symbols.

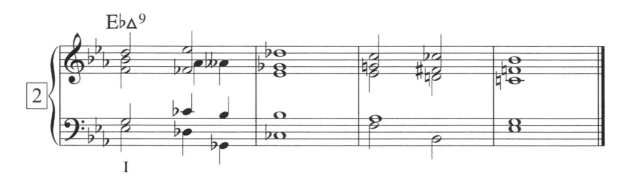

2. Transform the following ii—V⁷—I progressions using *Coltrane* substitutions and realize with "drop 2" five-part voicings.

EXPLORE THE POSSIBILITIES

3. Using a different key for each progression (as indicated), realize the following four-bar harmonic schemas in five-part keyboard texture and label each chord with lead-sheet symbols.

(1) G major	I—vi	ii—V⁷	iii—vi	ii—V⁷
(2) C major	I—♯i°	ii—♯ii°	ii—♭VI⁷	(ii—V⁷)/IV
(3) F major	I	(ii—V⁷)/IV	IV	ii—V⁷
(4) B♭ major	I	[iiø—V⁷]/vi	(ii—V⁷)/IV	IV
(5) D major	I—IV	iii—♭VII⁷	vi—II⁷	ii—Tr/V
(6) E♭ major	I	IV—♯iv°	I—VI⁷	II⁷—V⁷
(7) A major	I—♭V⁷	IV⁷—♭VII⁷	I—VI⁷	II⁷—Tr/V
(8) A♭ major	I	♯iv°—iv	iii—VI⁷	ii—♭VII⁷
(9) E major	I	[iiø—V⁷]/iii	[iiø—V⁷]/♭III	ii—V⁷
(10) G major	I	(iiø—V⁷)/ii	ii	(iiø—V⁷)/vi
(11) F major	I	[ii—V⁷]/♭II	ii—V⁷	I
(12) B♭ major	I	[ii—V⁷]/♭VII	[ii—V⁷]/♭VI	ii—V⁷
(13) A major	I	(ii—V⁷)/♭VI	♭VI	ii—V⁷

4. Using a different key for each progression (as indicated), realize the following four-bar harmonic schemas in four-part chorale texture and label each chord with lead-sheet symbols.

(1) G major	ii—V^7	I—vi	[ii—V^7]/♭III	ii—Tr/V
(2) C major	ii—V^7	vi—II^7	iii—♭iii°	ii—V^7
(3) F major	ii—V^7	[ii—V^7]/♭III	[ii—V^7]/♭V	(ii—V^7)/VI
(4) B♭ major	ii—V^7	[ii—V^7]/II	vi—II^7	ii—Tr/V
(5) D major	ii$^\varnothing$—V^7	I	[ii—V^7]/III	ii—V^7
(6) E♭ major	ii$^\varnothing$—V^7	I—♭V^7	IV^7—♭VII^7	I
(7) A major	(ii$^\varnothing$—V^7)/iv	iv	ii—V^7	I

5. Using a different key for each progression (as indicated), realize the following four-bar harmonic schemas in four-part chorale texture and label each chord using lead-sheet notation.

(1) A major	IV	[ii—V^7]/♭III	I	ii—Tr/V
(2) A♭ major	IV	ii—V^7	I—vi	(ii$^\varnothing$—V^7)/vi
(3) E major	IV	iii—vi	ii—V^7	Tr/V
(4) G major	IV	♯iv°	I	I
(5) F major	IV	[ii$^\varnothing$—V^7]/iii	(ii$^\varnothing$—V^7)/ii	ii—Tr/V
(6) B♭ major	IV	(ii$^\varnothing$—V^7)/vi	vi—II^7	ii—V^7

6. Using a different key for each progression (as indicated), realize the following four-bar harmonic schemas in five-part chorale texture and label each chord with lead-sheet symbols.

(1) B♭ major	vi	ii	V^7	I
(2) D major	vi	II^7	ii	Tr/V
(3) E♭ major	vi	ii—V^7	I	(ii$^\varnothing$—V^7)/ii
(4) A major	vi	[ii$^\varnothing$—V^7]/vi	(ii$^\varnothing$—V^7)/iii	iii
(5) A♭ major	vi	[ii$^\varnothing$—V^7]/vi	[ii—V^7]/IV	ii—V^7

CHAPTER 14

Bebop Improvisation

FUNDAMENTALS TO MASTERY

1. Between which scale degrees does the chromatic passing note occur in major bebop?

2. Between which scale degrees does the chromatic passing note occur in dominant bebop?

3. What are the melodic and harmonic ramifications of using the chromatic passing note in bebop scales?

4. Explain the relationship between intermediary and dominant bebop scales.

5. List all the pitch alterations that can potentially occur in altered bebop scales.

6. Discuss the relationship between the diminished 7th chord and major bebop.

7. Using bebop scales, establish a chord–scale relationship for the m7(♭5) and ø7 chords.

TEST YOUR KNOWLEDGE

1. Notate the pitches for the following bebop scales.

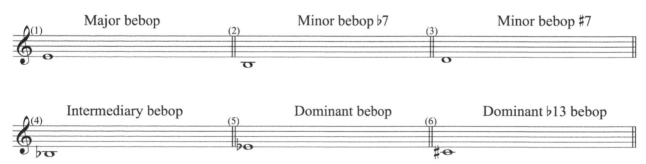

2. Identify the following bebop scales.

3. Using bebop scales, establish a convincing chord–scale relationship for the following chord progressions.

EXPLORE THE POSSIBILITIES

4. Compose an eight-bar bebop line for each of the following chords:

   a.   B♭7

   b.   E♭7(♯11)

   c.   DM9

   d.   D7(♭9)

   e.   Am7

   f.   Gm7(♭5)

   g.   F7alt

   h.   Em6/9

CHAPTER 15

Bebop Blues

FUNDAMENTALS TO MASTERY

1. Explain the role of harmonic rhythm in jazz composition.

2. How does the rate of harmonic rhythm affect jazz improvisation?

3. Tabulate the most common substitutions for mm. 1–4 of the blues and analyze their harmonic structure.

4. Compare and contrast harmonic progressions of "Billie's Bounce" and "Blues for Alice."

5. Provide a definition of the back-door dominant 7th. Describe its origins and analyze different harmonic contexts in which that chord can potentially occur. Find five examples from the jazz literature.

6. Explain the origins of chromatic [ii—V⁷]/X in the "Dance of the Infidels."

EXPLORE THE POSSIBILITIES

1. Beginning on the given pitch, compose a structural line and flesh it out with incomplete five-part chords using different arpeggiating patterns.[1] Provide a contextual harmonic analysis of your chord selection, label each chord with lead-sheet symbols, and perform the melodic line on your instrument.

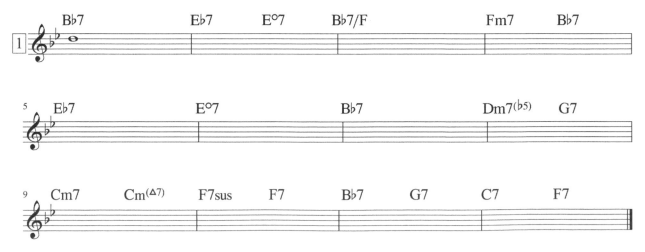

2. Based on the following blues progressions, compose a background line that uses "entry windows" between adjacent chords. Elaborate that line with melodic ideas typical of the bebop style.[2] Perform on your instrument.

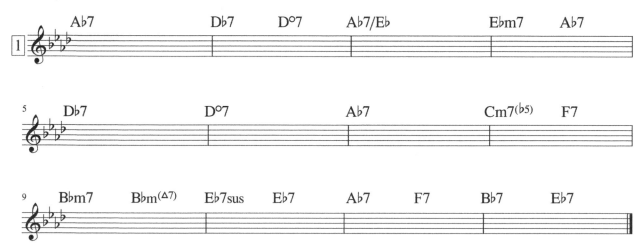

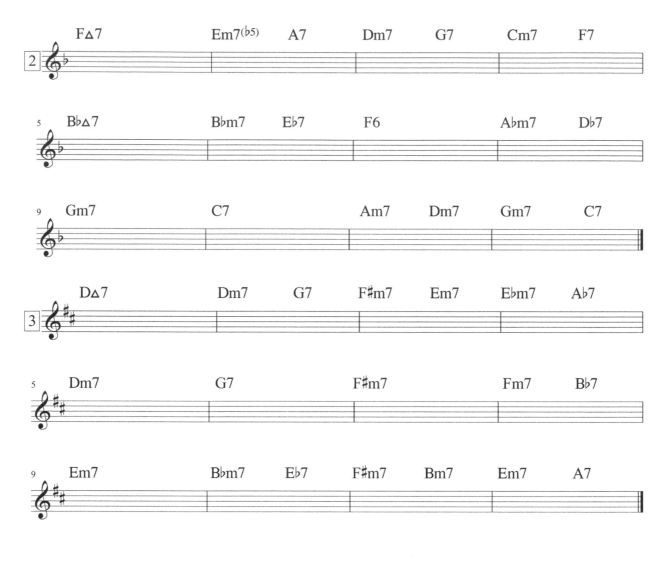

NOTES

1. See Figure 15.9 in *Jazz Theory—From Basic to Advanced Study.*
2. See Figure 15.10 in *Jazz Theory—From Basic to Advanced Study.*

CHAPTER 16

The "Confirmation" Changes

FUNDAMENTALS TO MASTERY

1. Explain the difference between a harmonically open and harmonically closed progression.

2. Describe the process of musical analysis. Which elements of the musical fabric lend themselves to analysis?

3. Discuss two contrasting methods of analytical inquiry.

TRANSCRIPTION

From the list below, select a solo and make a transcription. Analyze your transcription using various analytical strategies described in Chapters 16 and 19 in *Jazz Theory—From Basic to Advanced Study* and elsewhere.

- "Struttin' With Some Barbecue"—Louis Armstrong from *Louis Armstrong & His Hot Fives* (1927).

- "Potato Head Blues"—Louis Armstrong from *Louis Armstrong & His Hot Sevens* (1927).

- "Singin' the Blues"—Bix Beiderbecke from *Bix & Tram* (1927).

- "Lady Be Good"—Lester Young from *The Lester Young Story* (1936).

- "Lester Leaps In"—Lester Young from *Ken Burns Jazz: Lester Young* (1939).

- "Body and Soul"—Coleman Hawkins from *Body and Soul* (1939).

- "Embraceable You"—Charlie Parker from *Best of the Complete Savoy & Dial Studio Recordings* (1947).

- "Celia"—Bud Powell from *Jazz Giants* (1950).

- "Perdido"—Oscar Pettiford from *Great Times!* (1950).

- "Body and Soul"—Jack Teagarden from *Louis Armstrong—The California Concerts* (1951).

- "All the Things You Are"—Lee Konitz from *Lee Konitz & Gerry Mulligan* (1953).

- "Rocky Scotch"—Bob Brookmeyer from *The Dual Role of Bob Brookmeyer* (1954).

- "Sandu"—Clifford Brown from *Study in Brown* (1955).

- "A Gal in Calico"—Israel Crosby from *Ahmad Jamal Trio* (1955).

- "Ahmad's Blues"—Red Garland from *Workin'* (1956).

- "Caravan"—Kenny Drew from *Kenny Drew Trio* (1956).

- "St. Thomas"—Sonny Rollins from *Saxophone Colossus* (1956).

- "I Know That You Know"—Sonny Rollins from *Sonny Side Up* (1957).

- "Dear Old Stockholm"—Miles Davis from *Round About Midnight* (1957).

- "My Ideal"—Kenny Dorham from *Quiet Kenny* (1959).

- "Freddie Freeloader"—Wynton Kelly and Miles Davis from *Kind of Blue* (1959).

- "So What"—Miles Davis from *Kind of Blue* (1959).

- "Gone With the Wind"—Wes Montgomery from *Incredible Jazz Guitar of Wes Montgomery* (1960).

- "Remember"—Hank Mobley from *Soul Station* (1960).

- "I'll Close My Eyes"—Blue Mitchell from *Blue's Moods* (1960).

- "Autumn Leaves"—Ron Carter from *The Bobby Timmons Trio in Person* (1961).

- "Solar"—Bill Evans from *The Village Vanguard Sessions* (1961).

- "Ceora"—Hank Mobley from *Cornbread* (1965).

- "Fly Little Bird Fly"—McCoy Tyner from *Mustang* (1966).

- "Verse"—Joe Henderson from *Stick-Up!* (1966).

TEST YOUR KNOWLEDGE

1. Using modal scales, establish a chord–scale relationship for "Confirmation" in C.

2. Using bebop scales, establish a chord–scale relationship for "Confirmation" in E♭.

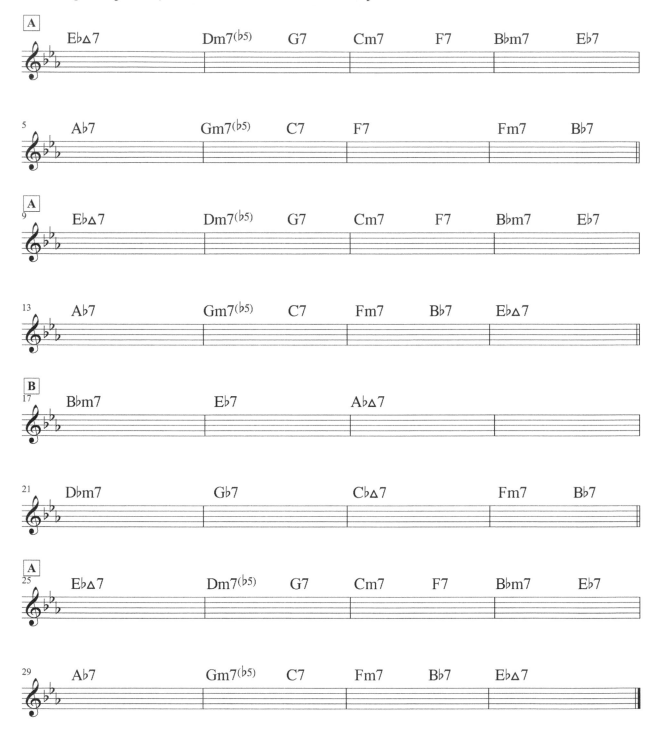

The Rhythm Changes

FUNDAMENTALS TO MASTERY

1. Define a contrafact. Provide three examples from the jazz literature.

2. Explain the difference between a melodic and harmonic contrafact. Provide examples from the jazz literature.

3. Name the five most popular harmonic progressions from standard tunes that jazz composers have often borrowed for contrafact compositions. Provide examples from the jazz literature.

4. What kind of harmonic progression is referred to as an eight-bar blues? Provide an example from the jazz literature.

5. Explain the difference between meter and hypermeter.

6. Provide three alternate sets of substitute chords for the A section of rhythm changes.

7. Provide three alternate sets of substitute chords for the B section of rhythm changes.

8. Which single bebop scale fits the content of mm. 1–4 of rhythm changes?

9. What harmonic challenges does one encounter in m. 5 of the rhythm changes progression?

10. What type of a cadence occurs at the end of the first A section of the rhythm changes composition?

11. Compare and contrast linear versus vertical approaches to jazz improvisation.

TEST YOUR KNOWLEDGE

1. Using one bebop scale only, compose eight-bar phrases for the following progressions.

2. Using two bebop scales, compose eight-bar phrases for the following progressions.

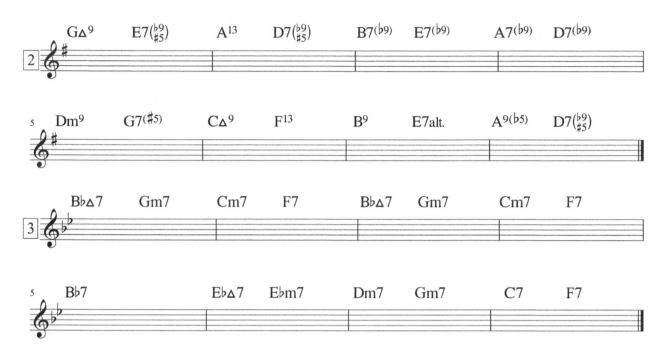

EXPLORE THE POSSIBILITIES

3. Using rhythm changes as the harmonic foundation, compose a melodic contrafact in B♭ major with melodic and rhythmic characteristics typical of the bebop style.

4. Using "Confirmation" changes as the harmonic foundation, compose a melodic contrafact in F major with melodic and rhythmic characteristics typical of the bebop style.

CHAPTER 18

Pentatonics, Hexatonics, Octatonics

FUNDAMENTALS TO MASTERY

1. What does the term "cardinality" mean?

2. What are the main characteristics of the Dorian pentatonic?

3. Explain the difference between altered and chromatic pentatonics.

4. What are the pros and cons of using the pentatonic system in jazz improvisation and harmony?

5. What style of jazz improvisation is likely to use pentatonic scales?

6. Describe the methodology of generating pentatonic voicings.

7. Describe the main characteristics of a palindromic structure (linear and vertical).

8. Discuss the harmonic and functional potential of quartal structures derived from the following pentatonic scales:

    a.   G Dorian

    b.   A Phrygian

    c.   D Mixolydian

    d.   D♭ Lydian

    e.   B♭ Aeolian

9. Describe the origins and the practical application of the "So What" voicings.

10. Explain the methodology of generating hexatonic scales.

11. Analyze the pitch content of Mixolydian ♭9 hexatonic. Which harmonic formation establishes a convincing chord–scale relationship with that hexatonic?

12. Explain the methodology of generating hexatonic voicings.

13. What special properties do "Modes of Limited Transposition" have?

14. What does the label "1/2" stand for in the "1/2 octatonic"?

15. How many unique transpositions does Mode 1 of Limited Transposition have? What is the recurring intervallic pattern in that scale? Name at least three chords that establish a convincing chord–scale relationship with Mode 1.

16. How many unique transpositions does Mode 2 of Limited Transposition have? What is the recurring intervallic pattern in that scale? Name at least three chords that establish a convincing chord–scale relationship with Mode 2.

17. How many unique transpositions does Mode 3 of Limited Transposition have? What is the recurring intervallic pattern in that scale? Name at least three chords that establish a convincing chord–scale relationship with Mode 3.

18. How many unique transpositions does Mode 4 of Limited Transposition have? What is the recurring intervallic pattern in that scale? Name at least three chords that establish a convincing chord–scale relationship with Mode 4.

19. How many unique transpositions does Mode 5 of Limited Transposition have? What is the recurring intervallic pattern in that scale? Name at least three chords that establish a convincing chord–scale relationship with Mode 5.

20. How many unique transpositions does Mode 6 of Limited Transposition have? What is the recurring intervallic pattern in that scale? Name at least three chords that establish a convincing chord–scale relationship with Mode 6.

21. How many unique transpositions does Mode 7 of Limited Transposition have? What is the recurring intervallic pattern in that scale? Name at least three chords that establish a convincing chord–scale relationship with Mode 7.

22. Describe the structure and functional behaviors of the double-diminished 7th chord.

23. Establish a chord–scale relationship for the double-diminished 7th chord.

24. Compare and contrast a bebop versus modal approach to jazz improvisation.

TEST YOUR KNOWLEDGE

1. Notate the following pentatonic scales.

2. Identify the following pentatonic scales.

3. Using the initial pentatonic formation, create a collection of pentatonic voicings.

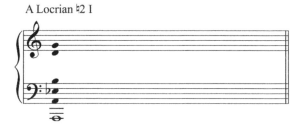

G Dominant   D Melodic Minor

F Altered   A Locrian ♮2 I

4. Notate the following hexatonic scales.

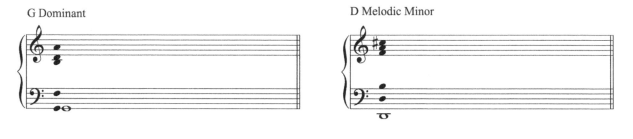

5. Identify the following hexatonic scales.

6. Using the initial hexatonic formation, create a collection of hexatonic voicings.

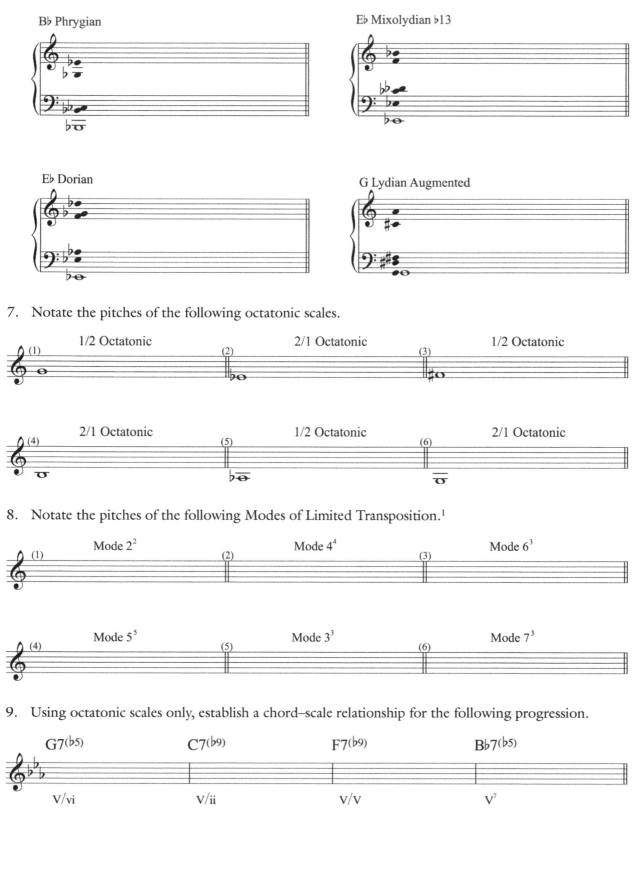

B♭ Phrygian

E♭ Mixolydian ♭13

E♭ Dorian

G Lydian Augmented

7. Notate the pitches of the following octatonic scales.

(1) 1/2 Octatonic   (2) 2/1 Octatonic   (3) 1/2 Octatonic

(4) 2/1 Octatonic   (5) 1/2 Octatonic   (6) 2/1 Octatonic

8. Notate the pitches of the following Modes of Limited Transposition.[1]

(1) Mode 2[2]   (2) Mode 4[4]   (3) Mode 6[3]

(4) Mode 5[5]   (5) Mode 3[3]   (6) Mode 7[3]

9. Using octatonic scales only, establish a chord–scale relationship for the following progression.

G7(♭5)   C7(♭9)   F7(♭9)   B♭7(♭5)

V/vi   V/ii   V/V   V[7]

EXPLORE THE POSSIBILITIES

10. For each of the following pentatonic scales, compose a 16-bar modal phrase:

   a.   D Dorian

   b.   G Phrygian

   c.   F♯ Aeolian

11. For each of the following hexatonic scales, compose a 16-bar modal phrase:

   a.   E Mixolydian ♭9

   b.   C♯ Melodic Minor

   c.   F Locrian ♮2

12. Compose a modal piece (32-bar AABA) based on the following harmonic structure:

   A (mm. 1–8)—GM9(♯11)

   A (mm. 9–16)—A♭M9(♯11)

   B (mm. 17–24)—B♭m(♯7)

   A (mm. 25–32)—C7sus(♭9)

13. Using the Modes of Limited Transposition, compose a modal piece according to the following formal guidelines:

   A (mm. 1–8)—Mode 2^1

   A (mm. 9–16)—Mode 2^1

   B (mm. 17–24)—Mode 4^2

   A (mm. 25–32)—Mode 2^2

14. Using the Modes of Limited Transposition, compose a modal piece according to the following formal guidelines:

   A (mm. 1–8)—Mode 2^2

   A (mm. 9–16)—Mode 2^2

   B (mm. 17–24)—Mode 6^1

   A (mm. 25–32)—Mode 4^2

NOTE

1. In keeping with Messiaen's nomenclature used in his theoretical writings, the Modes of Limited Transposition are labeled using two sets of Arabic numbers: (1) regular size numbers from 1 to 7 indicate seven modes, and (2) Arabic numbers in superscript indicate the transposition of a mode. For instance, Mode 1 (whole-tone scale) comes in two distinct transpositions, which will be notated as Mode 1^1 and Mode 1^2. Mode 2 (with the recurring intervallic pattern of minor and major 2nds: 1/2) comes in three transpositions, which will be labeled as Mode 2^1 (on C), Mode 2^2 (on C♯), and Mode 2^3 (on D). Mode 3 (with the intervallic pattern of 2/1/1) has four transpositions: 3^1 (on C), 3^2 (on C♯), 3^3 (on D), and 3^4 (on E♭). Mode 4 (with the intervallic pattern of 1/1/3/1) has six transpositions: 4^1 (on C), 4^2 (on C♯), 4^3 (on D), 4^4 (on E♭), 4^5 (on E), and 4^6 (on F). Mode 5 (with the intervallic pattern of 1/4/1) has six transpositions: 5^1 (on C), 5^2 (on C♯), 5^3 (on D), 5^4 (on E♭), 5^5 (on E), and 5^6 (on F). Mode 6 (with the intervallic pattern of 2/2/1/1) has six transpositions: 6^1 (on C), 6^2 (on C♯), 6^3 (on D), 6^4 (on E♭), 6^5 (on E), and 6^6 (on F). Mode 7 (with the intervallic pattern of 1/1/1/2/1) has six transpositions: 7^1 (on C), 7^2 (on C♯), 7^3 (on D), 7^4 (on E♭), 7^5 (on E), and 7^6 (on F).

CHAPTER 19

The *Tristano Style* of Improvisation

FUNDAMENTALS TO MASTERY

1. Describe the main characteristics of the *Tristano Style* of improvisation.

2. Explain the technique of rhythmic displacement. Demonstrate on your instrument.

3. How does the use of rhythmic displacement affect the rhythmic organization of an improvised solo?

4. How does the use of cross rhythm impact jazz improvisation? Provide an example.

5. What is the effect of melodic/harmonic interpolation in jazz improvisation?

6. What styles of jazz improvisation are likely to use the technique of playing outside?

7. How can the manipulation of harmonic rhythm be explored in jazz improvisation? Provide an example.

8. Compare and contrast the bebop style of improvisation with the *Tristano Style* of improvisation.

9. Explain the difference between formulaic and paraphrase improvisation. Identify jazz styles that are likely to explore these techniques of improvisation. Provide examples from the jazz literature.

EXPLORE THE POSSIBILITIES

1. Compose a contrafact in the *Tristano Style* based on the chord changes from the following standard tunes:

   a. "After You've Gone"—Layton & Creamer

   b. "There Is No Greater Love"—Jones & Symes

   c. "Sweet and Lovely"—Tobias & Arnheim

Advanced

PART THREE

CHAPTER 20

Analyzing Jazz Lead Sheets

MASTERY TO EXCELLENCE

1. What is a lead sheet? What kinds of musical information does it contain?

2. What does the term "fake" in the "fake book" stand for?

3. What types of musical compositions are typically compiled in the fake book?

4. Describe the method of musical inquiry knows as a two-level analysis.

5. What types of musical events are subject to the first level of musical analysis?

6. What types of musical events are subject to the second level of musical analysis?

7. Explain the difference between a structural and tonicizing ii—V^7 progression.

8. Examine different types of analytical tools that are frequently implemented in a two-level analysis.

9. Describe the role of an incomplete ii—V^7 progression in standard tunes.

10. Discuss the concept of monotonality and its role in common-practice music.

11. What is the difference between structural versus embellishing chords? Provide an example.

MUSICAL ANALYSIS

1. Using a two-level analysis, analyze the following standard tunes:

   a. "How Deep Is the Ocean"—Berlin

   b. "Old Folks"—Robison & Hill

   c. "I Wish I Knew"—Warren & Gordon

   d. "So In Love"—Porter

   e. "That Certain Feeling"—Gershwin & Gershwin

Phrase Models

MASTERY TO EXCELLENCE

1. What musical properties do phrase models attempt to codify?

2. Examine the function of the three structural components of phrase models.

3. Which part of the phrase model has the most harmonic variables deeming it difficult to formalize?

4. Describe the interaction between counterpoint, harmony, and meter in standard tunes.

5. Compare and contrast the use of phrase models in jazz to the use of galant schematas in classical compositions.

6. Describe each phrase model discussed in Chapter 21 of *Jazz Theory—From Basic to Advanced Study* and provide the name of two standard tunes that fit its harmonic design.

7. What types of cadential gestures are likely to be found in standard tunes?

8. Explain the difference between an on-tonic and off-tonic phrase model. For each type, provide two examples from the jazz literature.

9. What kind of a phrase model is known as the incomplete? Provide two examples from the jazz literature.

10. What is the relationship between the contrapuntal framework and fully fledged harmonic progression of a standard tune?

11. Discuss the role of the Rule of the Octave during the Baroque period.

12. Compare and contrast the use of the Rule of the Octave in Baroque versus jazz music.

13. What specific lessons can be learned from analyzing the different settings of the jazz Rule of the Octave shown in the book?

14. Explain the influence of phrase identifiers on the overall unfolding of chord progressions in standard tunes. Provide an example.

15. Which chromatic phrase model can be used as an effective harmonic substitute for a diatonic phrase model? What specific conditions have to be met in order for that substitution to be successfully implemented?

16. Explain the relationship between melody and meter and their influence on the formation of harmonic progressions in standard tunes.

17. What are the pedagogical benefits of learning standard tunes using the concept of phrase models?

TEST YOUR KNOWLEDGE

1. Using the concept of phrase models, identify the following eight-bar progressions. Analyze them with Roman numerals.

Autumn Leaves (mm. 9–16)

I Love You (mm. 1–8)

All the Things You Are (mm. 1–8)

My Romance (mm. 9–16)

EXPLORE THE POSSIBILITIES

2. Using the specified method of keyboard realization, provide harmonic settings for the following chord progressions. Where applicable, expand the structure of chords with chordal extensions and/ or pitch alterations. Maintain a good voice leading. Label each chord using the lead-sheet notation and identify each phrase model.

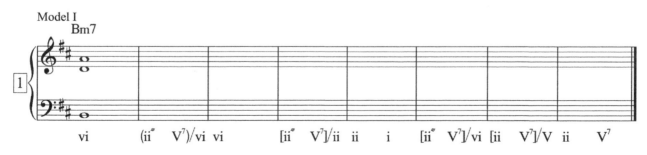

Model I

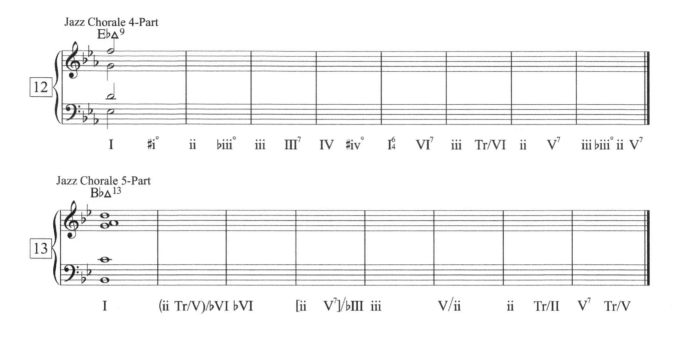

Jazz Chorale 4-Part
Eb△9

12

I   #i°   ii   biii°   iii   III⁷   IV   #iv°   I⁶₄   VI⁷   iii   Tr/VI   ii   V⁷   iii biii° ii V⁷

Jazz Chorale 5-Part
Bb△13

13

I   (ii Tr/V)/bVI bVI   [ii   V⁷]/bIII iii   V/ii   ii   Tr/II   V⁷   Tr/V

CHAPTER 22

Song Forms

MASTERY TO EXCELLENCE

1. Discuss the most popular formal designs found in standard tunes. Provide examples from the jazz literature.

2. Select a standard tune; find a lead sheet and an original sheet music for that song. Compare and contrast both versions. Which version of the song is more reliable and why?

3. What role does the verse play in standard tunes?

4. Provide the names of five composers who contributed to the development of the repertory of American standard tunes.

5. Name five lyricists who collaborated with composers in the creation of the American songbook.

6. What does the term "reached by arrival" mean?

7. Provide a definition of the harmonic interruption. Where does it typically occur in standard tunes? What is its formal function?

8. What is a sentence structure? Discuss its potential in jazz improvisation. Demonstrate on your instrument.

9. Speculate about possible reasons for a large number of tunes with the bridge in a subdominant.

10. Discuss the formal and tonal structure of a standard tune based on the 32-bar on-tonic AABA design. Provide three examples of standard tunes.

11. Discuss the formal and tonal structure of a standard tune based on the 32-bar off-tonic AABA design. Provide three examples of standard tunes.

12. Discuss the formal and tonal structure of a standard tune based on the 32-bar on-tonic ABAC design. Provide three examples of standard tunes.

13. Discuss the formal and tonal structure of a standard tune based on the 32-bar off-tonic ABAC design. Provide three examples of standard tunes.

14. Discuss the formal and tonal structure of a standard tune based on an unconventional formal design. Provide three examples of standard tunes.

MUSICAL ANALYSIS

1. Using the analyses of songs in the book as a model, analyze the following standard tunes:

    a. "It's You or No One"—Cahn & Styne

    b. "From This Moment On"—Porter

    c. "Days of Wine and Roses"—Mancini & Mercer

    d. "Love Walked In"—Gershwin & Gershwin

    e. "The Song Is You"—Kern & Hammerstein II

CHAPTER 23

Reharmonization Techniques

MASTERY TO EXCELLENCE

1. Discuss the role of reharmonization in jazz.

2. What specific conditions have to be met for a reharmonization to be successful?

3. Compare and contrast vertical versus horizontal approaches to reharmonization. Provide an example.

4. Select five basic reharmonization techniques discussed in the book and explain their *modus operandi*.

5. Discuss ways of implementing the technique of melodic recontextualization while reharmonizing standard tunes.

6. What is the impact of tonally different pedal points on jazz harmony, improvisation, and musical interaction between band members?

7. What are the benefits of using upper-structure triads in the process of reharmonization?

8. Who is credited with the development of harmonic style known as the block-chord style? What types of harmonic formations are likely to be implemented in this style?

9. Explain the use of cyclic harmony in jazz reharmonization.

10. What types of intervallic cycles are most prevalent in jazz reharmonization?

11. Discuss the characteristics of modal harmony and explore ways of implementing it in jazz reharmonization.

12. Select ten signature chords by different composers and demonstrate their potential in jazz reharmonization.

13. What is the role of outer-voice counterpoint in jazz reharmonization?

14. What specific properties should the outer-voice counterpoint possess in order to be useful in jazz reharmonization?

15. Discuss the role and origins of voice-leading chords. What is their role in jazz reharmonization?

EXPLORE THE POSSIBILITIES

1. Using diatonic extensions, expand the chord structure of the following tunes:

   a. "Beautiful Love"—Young & King

   b. "Darn That Dream"—Van Heusen & DeLange

   c. "Willow Weep for Me"—Ronell

2. Using chromatic extensions and pitch alterations, expand the chord structure of the following tunes:

   a. "There Will Never Be Another You"—Warren & Gordon

   b. "What's New"—Haggard & Burke

   c. "Moonlight in Vermont"—Suessdorf & Blackburn

3. Using tonicizations, tritone substitutions, and melodic recontextualizations, reharmonize the following tunes:

   a. "These Foolish Things"—Strachey & Link

   b. "Ain't Misbehavin'"—Waller & Brooks

   c. "What a Difference a Day Made"—Adams & Grever

4. Using linear techniques of reharmonization, modify the harmonic structure of the following tunes:

   a. "A Foggy Day"—Gershwin & Gershwin

   b. "Tenderly"—Gross & Lawrence

   c. "You're My Everything"—Warren & Dixon

5. Using modal and cyclic harmony, reharmonize the following standard tunes:

   a. "A Weaver of Dreams"—Young & Elliott

   b. "I've Never Been in Love Before"—Loesser

   c. "Memories of You"—Razaf & Blake

6. Using one signature chord (per tune) by a composer of your choice along with its logical transformations, reharmonize the following standards:

   a. "We'll Be Together Again"—Fischer & Laine

   b. "Day by Day"—Cahn & Stordahl

   c. "Mean to Me"—Turk & Ahlert

CHAPTER 24

Post-Tonal Jazz—Atonality

MASTERY TO EXCELLENCE

1. What are the fundamental differences between atonal and twelve-tone music?

2. Explain the difference between pitch and pitch class.

3. How many pitch classes are there and how are they labeled?

4. What is the difference between unordered and ordered intervals?

5. Explain the difference between interval and interval class.

6. How many interval classes are there and how are they labeled?

7. What kinds of transformations can be advanced using arithmetic modulo 12 (mod 12)?

8. Describe procedures for finding normal form.

9. Describe procedures for finding prime form.

10. Provide a definition of the interval-class vector.

11. What can be gleaned from analyzing the interval-class vector of a musical set?

12. Explain the difference between symmetrical and non-symmetrical set classes. Provide an example.

13. What does the index number represent?

14. Explain the procedures for comparing and establishing an intervallic relationship between transpositionally related set classes.

15. Explain the procedures for comparing and establishing an intervallic relationship between inversionally related set classes.

16. What does the term "mapping" mean?

17. Compare and contrast literal versus abstract relationships. Which one is more valuable for analytical purposes?

18. What properties are represented by integers in the magic square?

19. What are the main claims of atonal music theory?

TEST YOUR KNOWLEDGE

1. Using integer notation, write the following notes as pitches and pitch classes.

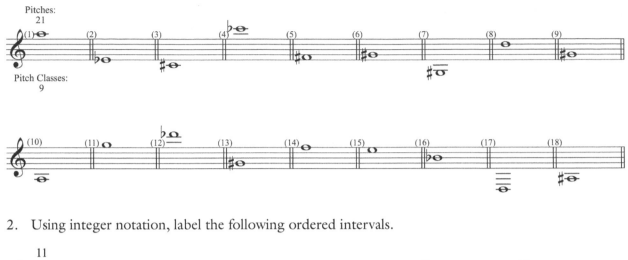

2. Using integer notation, label the following ordered intervals.

3. Using integer notation, label the following unordered intervals.

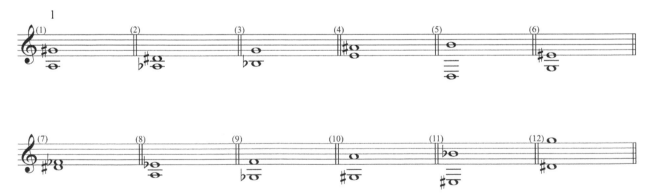

4. Put the following collections in normal form and calculate the interval-class vector.

5. Put the following collections in prime form and calculate the interval-class vector.

6. Transpose the following set classes by T₃:

   a. [2,5,9]

   b. [4,6,9]

   c. [5,6,e,0]

   d. [5,7,9,t]

7. Invert the following set classes by I_5:

   a. [1,4,8]

   b. [2,4,7]

   c. [6,7,0,1]

   d. [2,4,6,8]

8. Calculate the index number for the following transpositionally related pairs of set classes:

   a. [1,5,8] [9,1,4]

   b. [2,6,t] [5,9,1]

   c. [3,6,9] [2,5,8]

9. For each of the following sets, calculate the interval-class content and notate it as an interval-class vector:

   a. [1,5,4,t]

   b. [0,8,2]

   c. [2,5,6,8,e]

   d. [4,2,9,t]

10. Calculate the index number for the following inversionally related pairs of set classes:

    a. [1,4,8] [9,1,4]

    b. [0,2,6] [0,4,6]

    c. [0,4,5] [e,0,4]

11. Using movable do, sing the following melody.

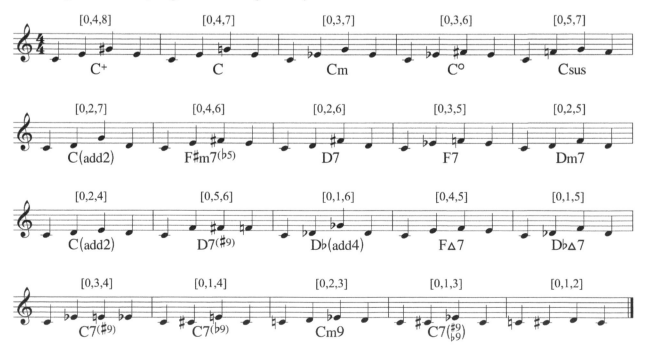

EXPLORE THE POSSIBILITIES

12. Using the chord structure of "Cherokee," compose a jazz contrafact based on the following guidelines:

    a. **A** Section—two trichords from the diatonic category of trichords in different T_n and I_n transformations

    b. **B** Section—two trichords from the semitonal category of trichords in different T_n and I_n transformations

CHAPTER 25

Set Classes in Jazz

MASTERY TO EXCELLENCE

1. List all the trichords that belong to the "triadic" category. Describe their potential use in jazz improvisation and composition.

2. List all the trichords that belong to the "whole-tone" category. Describe their potential use in jazz improvisation and composition.

3. List all the trichords that belong to the "diatonic" category. Describe their potential use in jazz improvisation and composition.

4. List all the trichords that belong to the "semitonal" category. Describe their potential use in jazz improvisation and composition.

5. What is the main characteristic of any pair of Z-related set classes? Provide an example.

6. Discuss the use of rotations in jazz improvisation.

7. Examine the properties of the all-interval vector. Select a pitch-class set with the all-interval vector and analyze its properties.

8. What does the term "combinatoriality" signify?

9. Speculate about pro and cons of using set classes in jazz improvisation and composition.

TEST YOUR KNOWLEDGE

1. Using the realization of (014) as a model, calculate the normal and prime forms for the remaining pitch-class collections. Explore their potential in terms of upper structures superimposed over major, minor, dominant, half-diminished, and diminished chords.

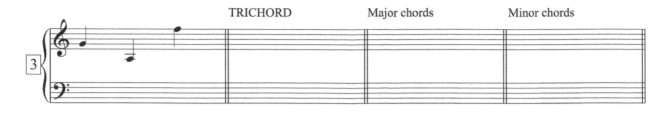

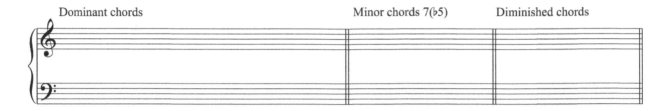

2. For each of the following tetrachords, calculate normal form, prime form, and an interval-class vector. Label each tetrachord with a Forte's number.

Normal form: [0,1,6,7]
Prime form: (0167)
Forte's name: 4-9

Inverval-class vector ICV:
[200022]

3. For each of the following pentachords, calculate normal form, prime form, and an interval-class vector. Label each pentachord with a Forte's number.

Normal form: [5,9,t,0,1]
Prime form: (01348)
Forte's name: 5-Z17
Interval-class vector ICV:
[212320]

4. For each of the following hexachords, calculate normal form, prime form, and an interval-class vector. Label each hexachord with a Forte's number.

Normal form: [6,7,8,9,t,e]
Prime form: (012345)
Forte's name: 6-1
Interval-class vector ICV:
    [543210]

5. For the following sets, calculate the number of common tones under transposition with each set transposed by T_3, T_5, and T_6:

    a. [3,1,2,5,9,7]

    b. [1,2,3,5,8,9]

    c. [t,8,1,5,3]

    d. [1,3,5,6,9]

6. For the following sets, create a magic square and calculate the number of common tones under inversion with each set inverted by I_3, I_6, and I_8:

    a. (013679)

    b. (012678)

    c. (01468)

    d. (01369)

    e. (0257)

    f. (0358)

EXPLORE THE POSSIBILITIES

7. Using two hexachords, (1) 6-Z17 (012478) and (2) 6–20 (014589), compose a piece for a jazz sextet (trumpet, tenor saxophone, trombone, and rhythm section).

CHAPTER 26

Twelve-Tone Techniques

MASTERY TO EXCELLENCE

1. What does the term "pitch aggregate" stand for?

2. What are the main contributions of the Third Stream movement in jazz?

3. What types of pitch relationships occur in twelve-tone music?

4. Describe different methods of labeling twelve-tone rows.

5. Explain the *modus operandi* of four canonic twelve-tone operations (TTOs).

6. What common characteristics do all-combinatorial hexachords possess?

7. In what way are the M and MI operations different from the canonic TTOs?

8. Explain the methodology of constructing a twelve-tone matrix.

9. Examine the relationship of intervals from an I-series in relation to a P-series.

10. Examine the relationship of intervals from a R-series in relation to a P-series.

11. Examine the relationship of intervals from a RI-series in relation to a P-series.

12. Examine the relationship of intervals from a RI-series in relation to an I-series.

13. Examine the relationship of intervals from a M-series in relation to a P-series.

14. Examine the relationship of intervals from a MI-series in relation to a P-series.

15. How many and which hexachords possess all-combinatorial properties?

16. Speculate about the possibility of using twelve-tone rows in jazz improvisation and composition.

TEST YOUR KNOWLEDGE

1. Transform the given twelve-tone rows using P_3, I_8, R_6, and RI_t.

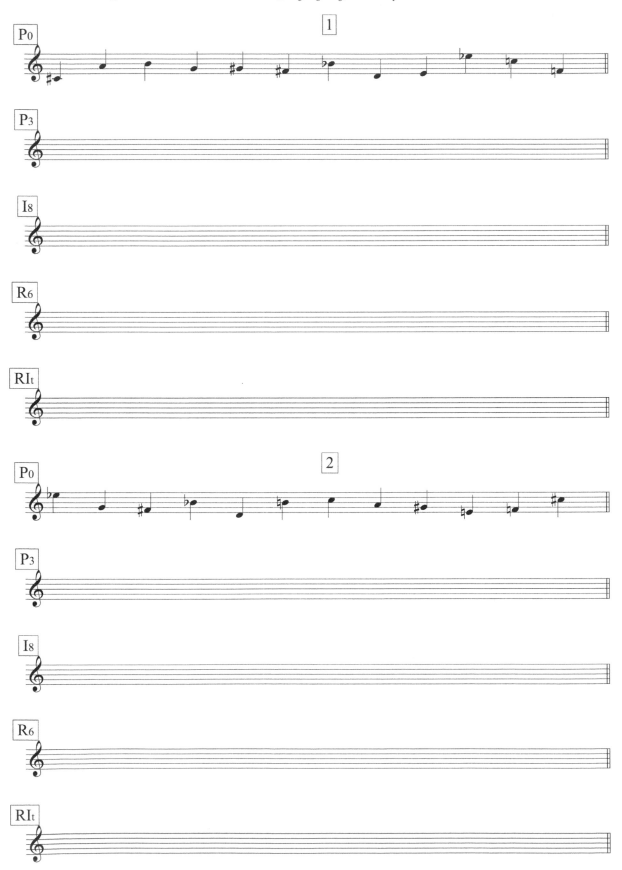

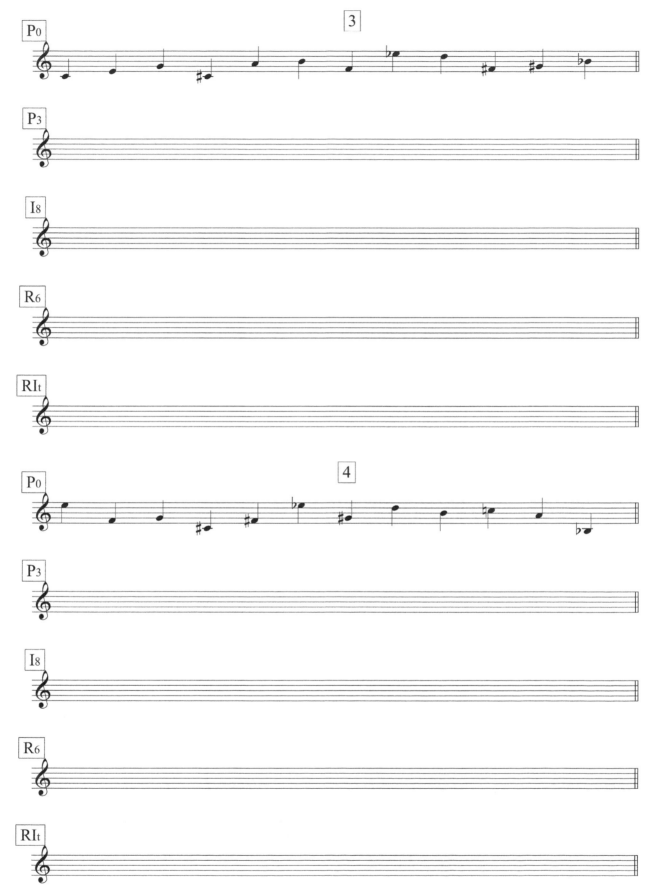

2. For each of the following twelve-tone rows, create a twelve-tone matrix.

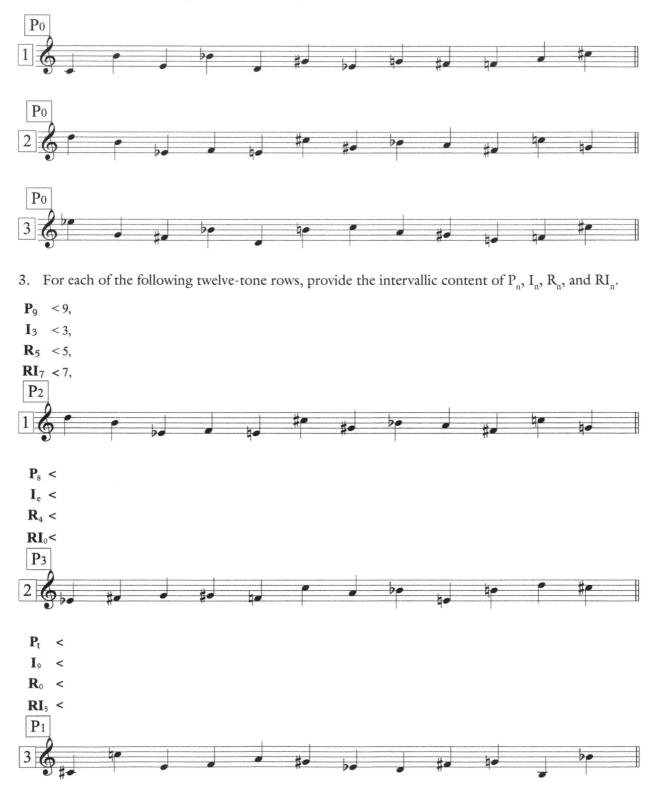

3. For each of the following twelve-tone rows, provide the intervallic content of P_n, I_n, R_n, and RI_n.

P_9 $< 9,$

I_3 $< 3,$

R_5 $< 5,$

RI_7 $< 7,$

P_8 $<$

I_e $<$

R_4 $<$

RI_0 $<$

P_t $<$

I_9 $<$

R_0 $<$

RI_5 $<$

4. Create a rotational array for the following hexachords.

   a.   [2,0,9,e,4,t]

   b.   [3,2,6,4,5,8]

   c.   [t,8,9,1,0,e]

EXPLORE THE POSSIBILITIES

5. For each of the following twelve-tone rows, compose a bass line using I_n, R_n, or RI_n. Realize the outer-voice framework with chords typical of the jazz syntax.

6. Using the following twelve-tone rows, compose a piece for a jazz quintet (trumpet, alto saxophone, and rhythm section).

CHAPTER 27

Stylistic Crossovers—Developing a New Jazz Repertory

MASTERY TO EXCELLENCE

1. What specific techniques and strategies can be advanced in the process of "deconstructing" standard tunes? Provide an example from the jazz literature.

2. Propose and describe your own methodology of developing a new jazz repertory.

EXPLORE THE POSSIBILITIES

1. Using various methods of developing a new jazz repertory (your own or from the book), deconstruct the following compositions and arrange them for a jazz ensemble (your choice of instrumentation). The scores can be found online at http://imslp.org/wiki/Main_Page.

    a. Italian Concerto, BWV. 971, i—J. S. Bach

    b. Sonata Pathetique, Op. 13, ii—L. Beethoven

    c. Prelude, Op. 28 No. 4—F. Chopin

    d. Piano Trio, Op. 99, ii—F. Schubert

    e. Piano Trio, Op. 63, iii—R. Schumann

    f. "Il pleure dans mon coeur" from *Ariettes oubliées*—C. Debussy

    g. Prelude, Op. 1 No. 1—K. Szymanowski

Appendix A
Rhythmic Exercises

MASTER THE FUNDAMENTALS

UNIT 1   4/4 Meter

Perform the following exercises with a metronome.

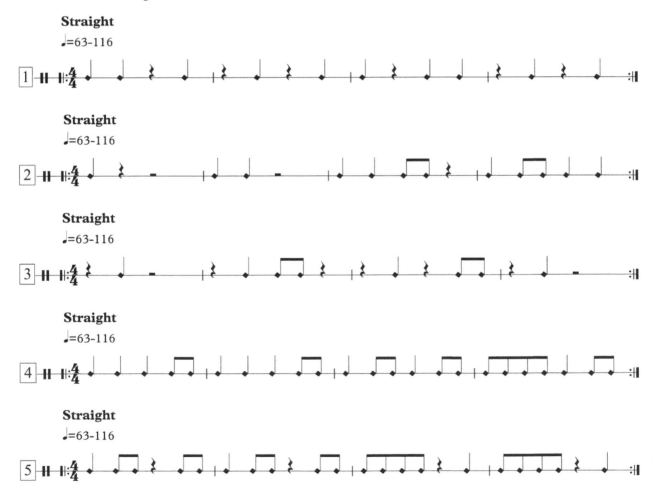

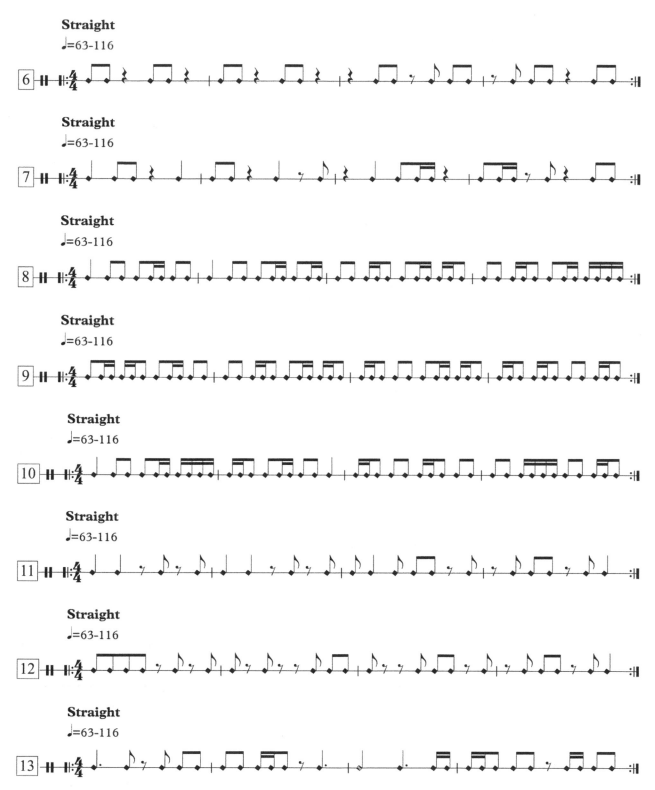

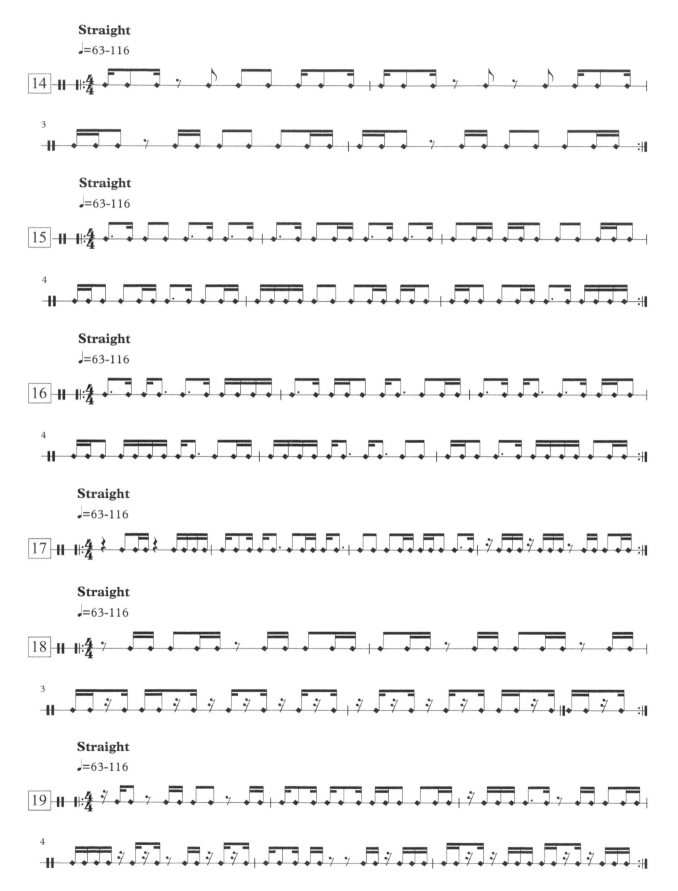

Straight

♩=50-120

UNIT 2   4/4 Meter With Triplets

Perform the following exercises with a metronome.

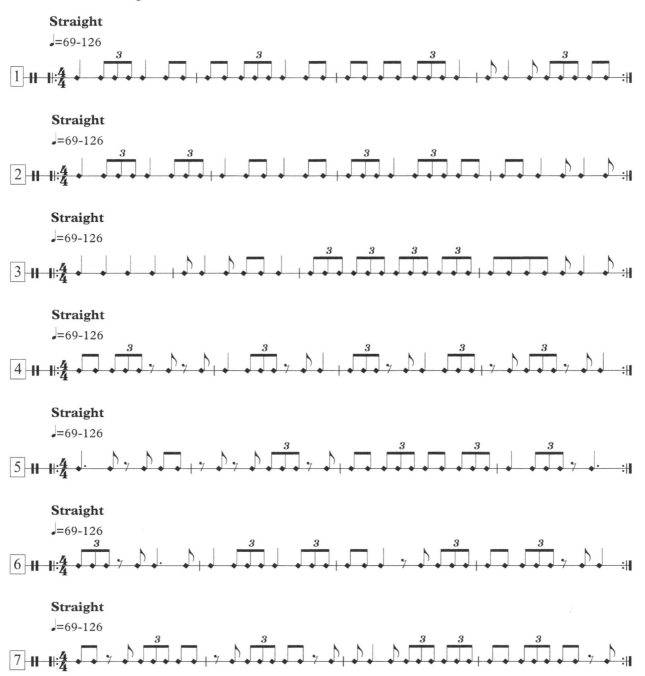

Straight

♩=69-126

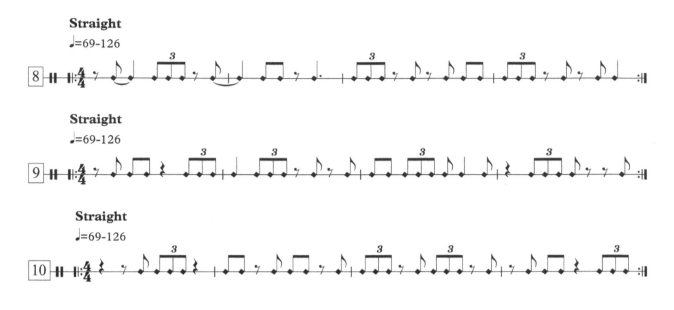

UNIT 3   3/4 Meter

Perform the following exercises with a metronome.

Straight

♩=72-116

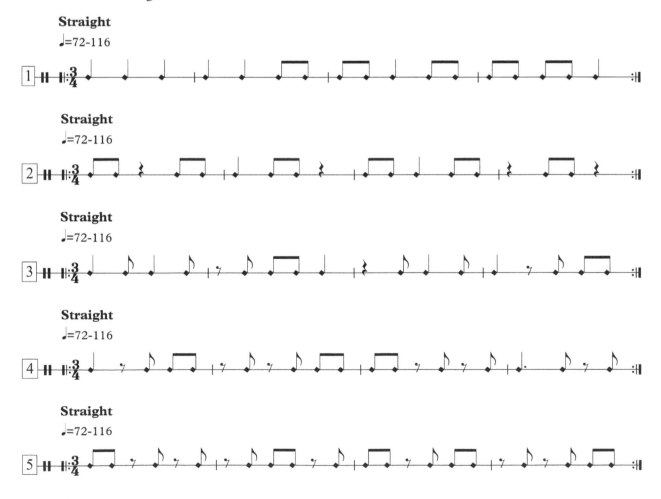

Straight

♩=72-116

UNIT 4   3/4 Meter With Triplets

Perform the following exercises with a metronome.

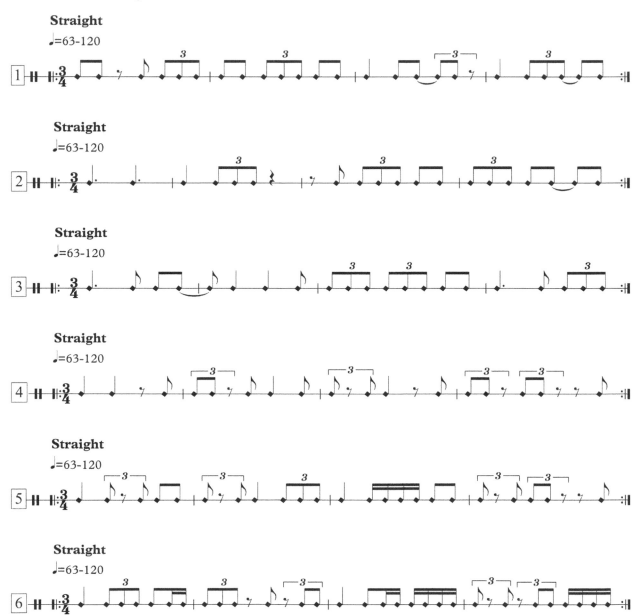

UNIT 5   6/8 Meter

Perform the following exercises with a metronome.

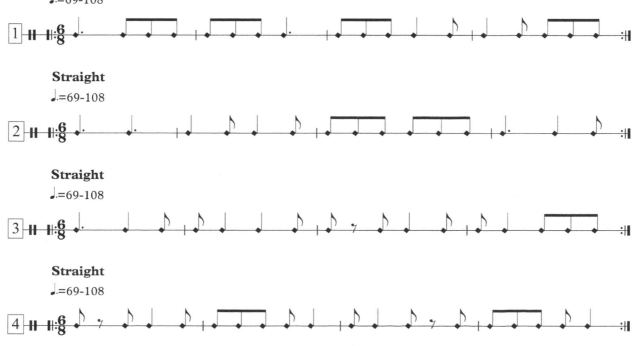

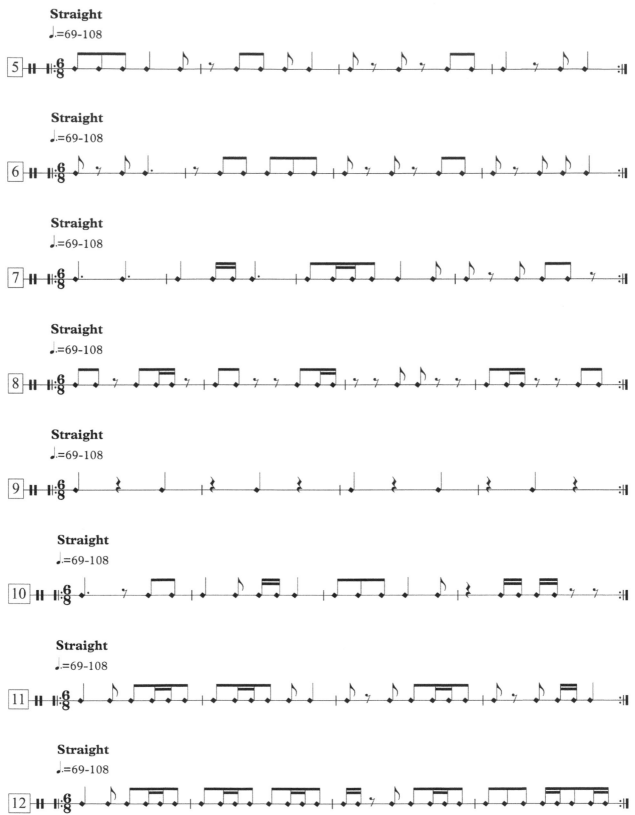

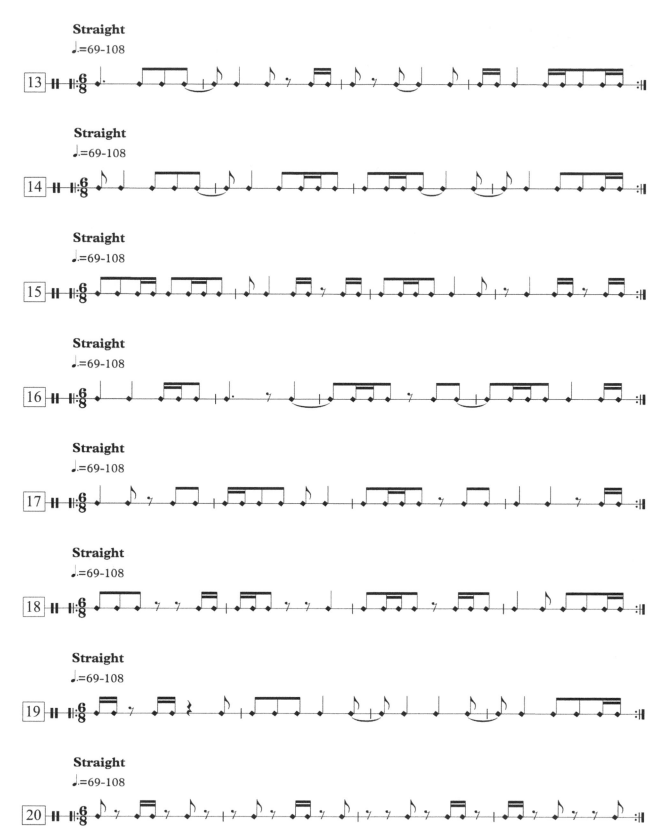

FUNDAMENTALS TO MASTERY

UNIT 6   4/4 Meter—Swing Rhythms

Perform the following exercises with a metronome on "two and four."[1]

UNIT 7   3/4 Meter—Swing Rhythms

Perform the following exercises with a metronome.

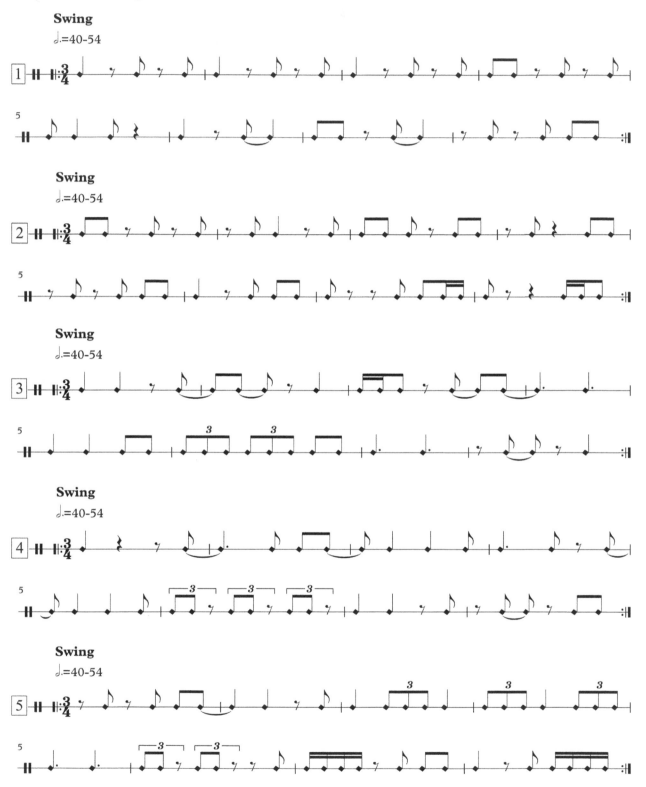

UNIT 8   5/4 Meter

Perform the following exercises with a metronome.

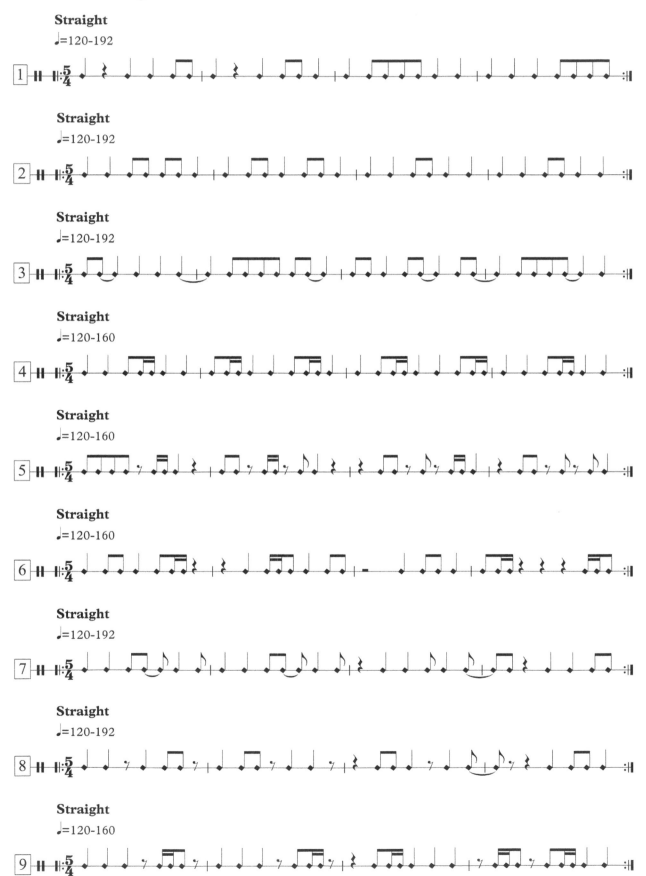

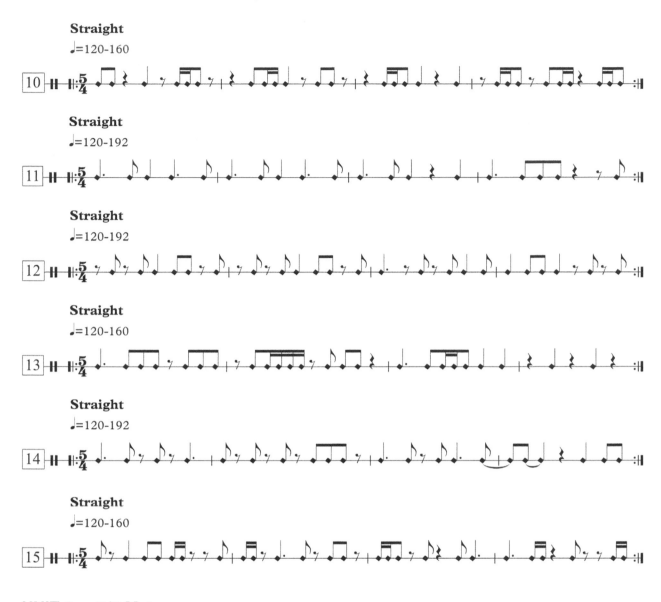

UNIT 9   7/8 Meter

Perform the following exercises with a metronome.

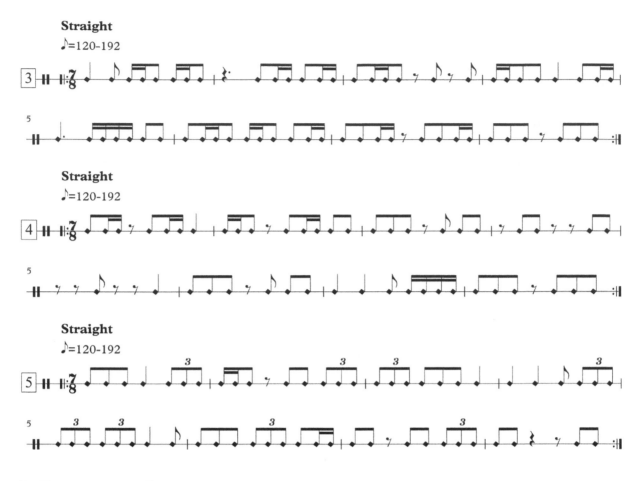

UNIT 10   Longer Exercises

Perform the following exercises with a metronome.

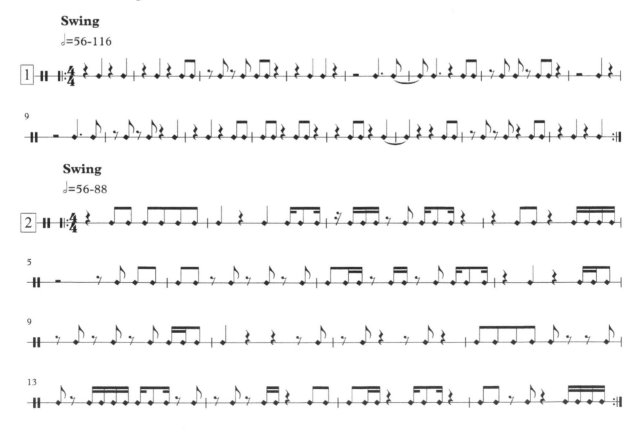

Swing

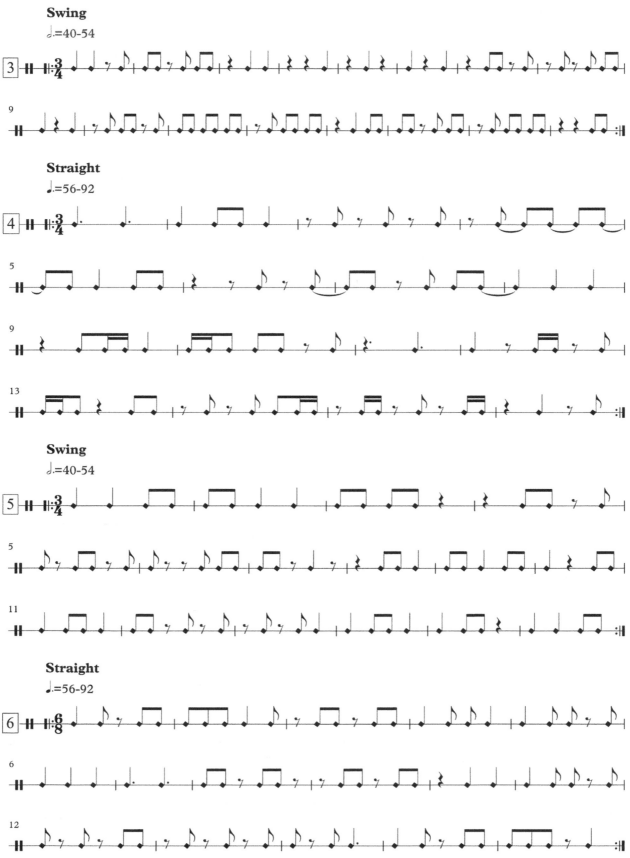

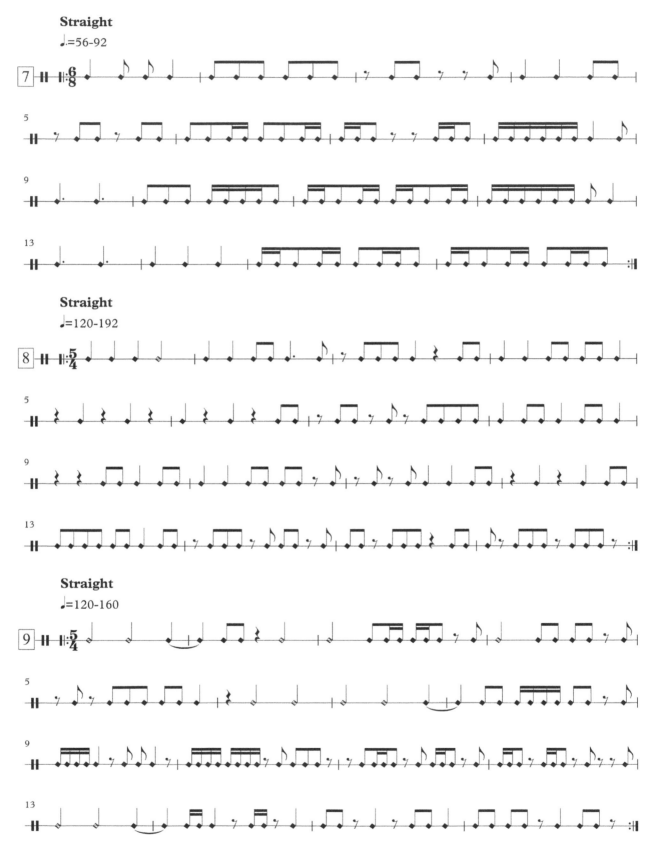

Straight

♩=120-192

MASTERY TO EXCELLENCE

UNIT 11   Two-Hand Rhythms

Perform the following exercises with a metronome.

Swing

♩=56-116

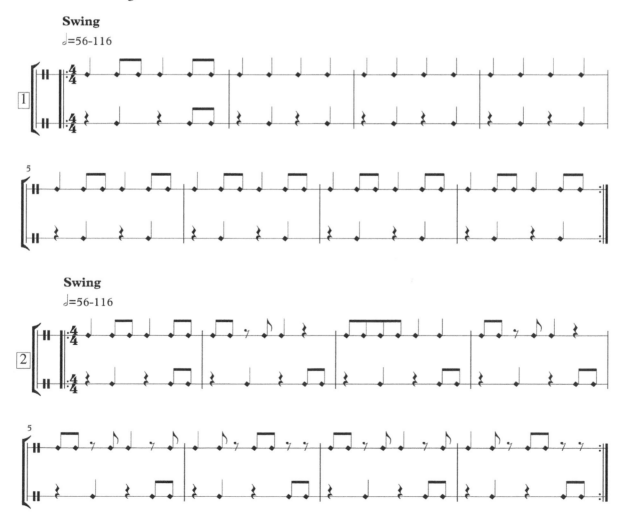

Swing

♩=56-116

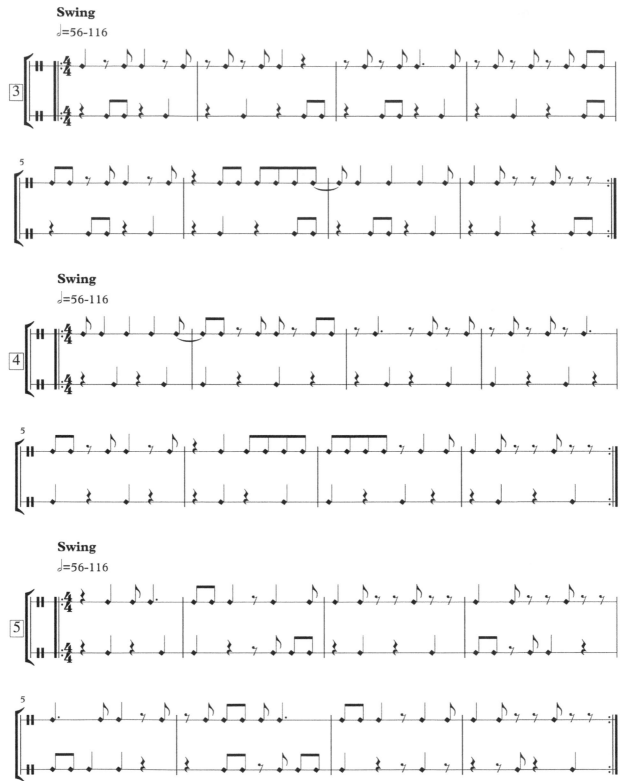

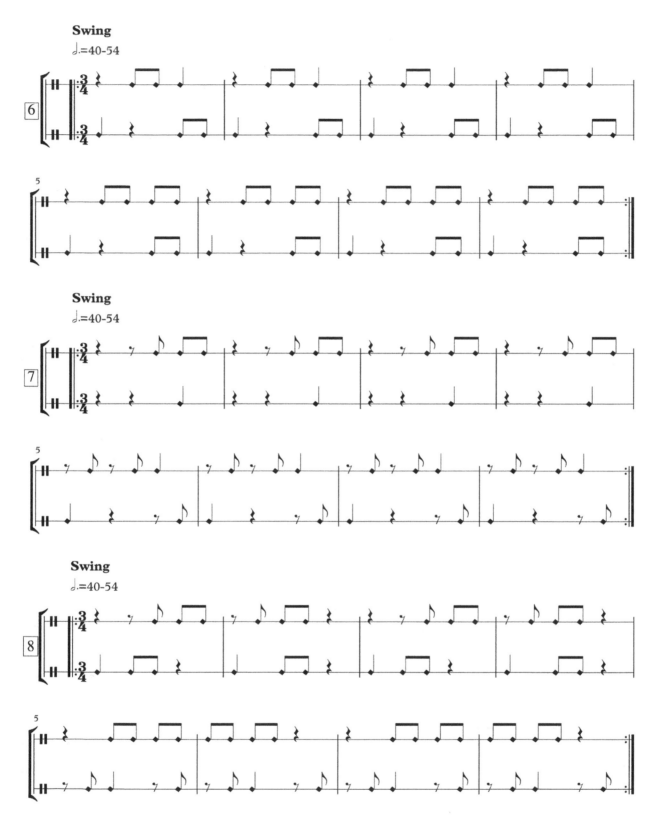

Swing

♩.=40-54

Swing

♩.=40-54

Straight

♩=60-120

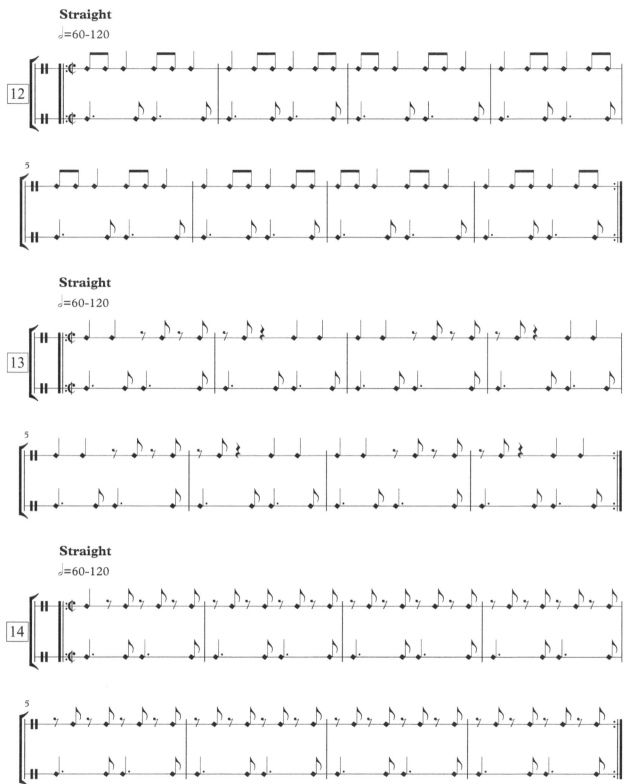

Straight

♩=60-120

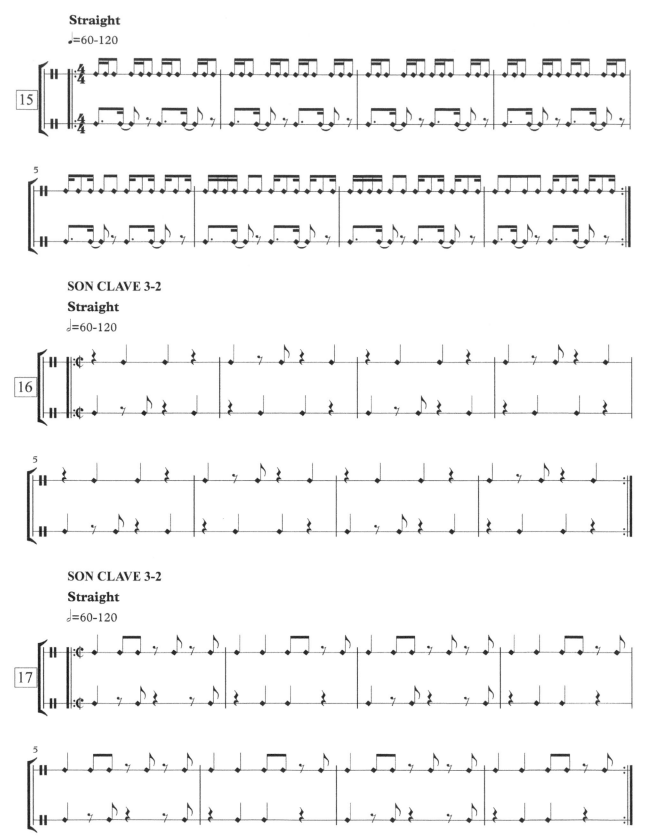

SON CLAVE 3-2

Straight

♩=60-120

SON CLAVE 3-2

Straight

♩=60-120

RUMBA CLAVE 3-2

Straight

♩=60-120

18

RUMBA CLAVE 2-3

Straight

♩.=69-112

19

SON CLAVE 3-2

Straight

♩=60-120

20

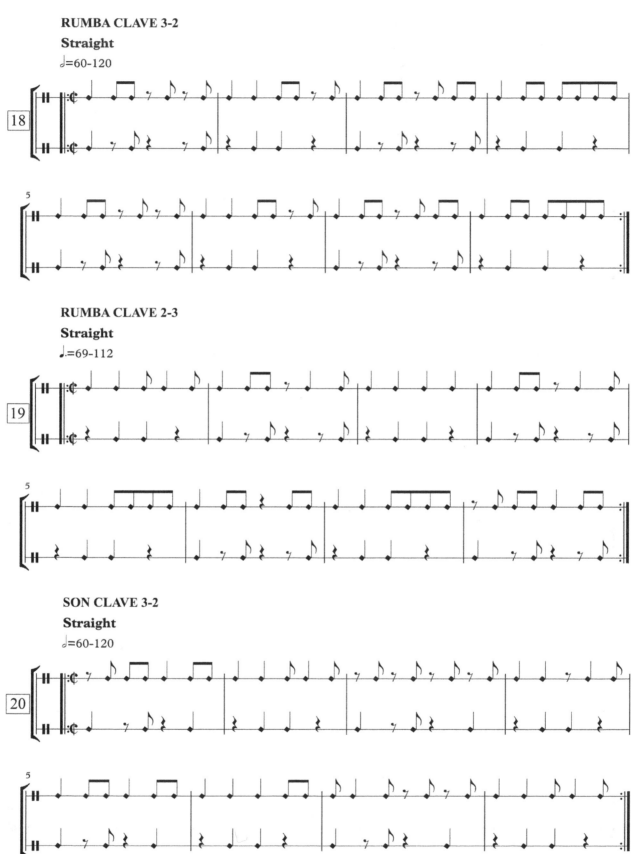

SON CLAVE 6/8 3-2

Straight

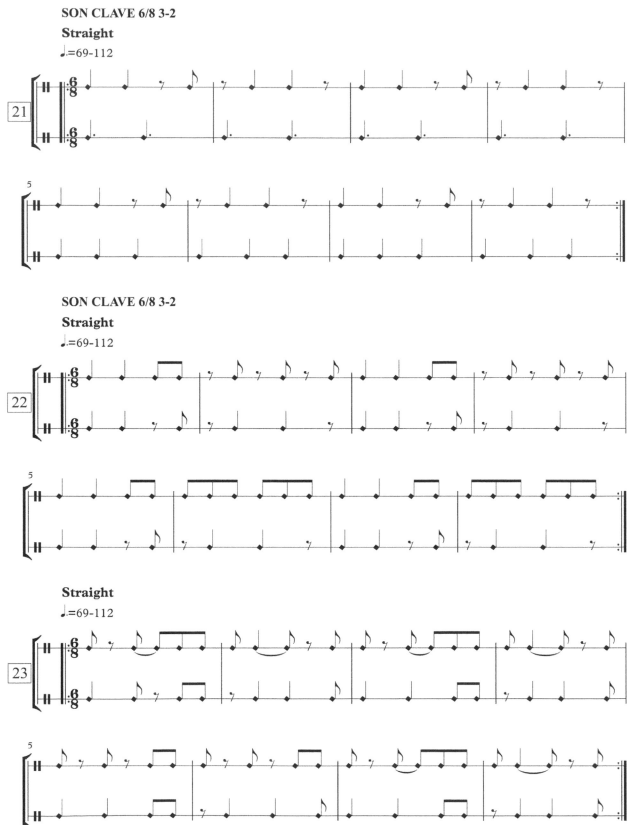

SON CLAVE 6/8 3-2

Straight

Straight

Straight

♩.=69-112

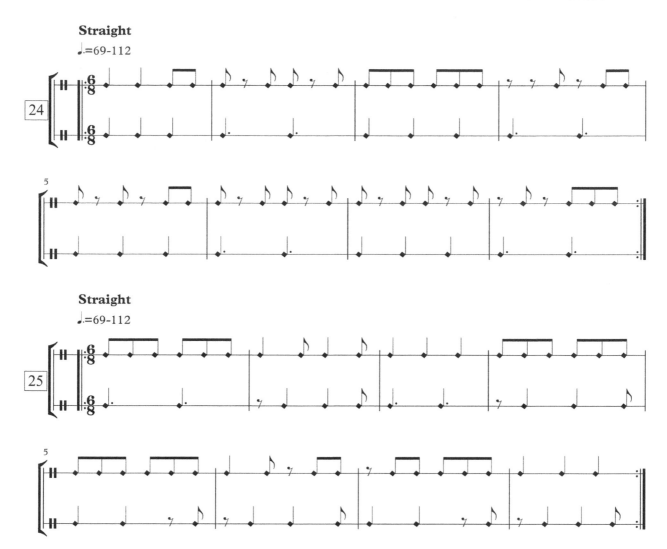

UNIT 12   Changing Meter

Perform the following exercises with a metronome.

Straight

♩ = ♩

♩=50-96

UNIT 13   Metric Modulations

Perform the following exercises.

NOTE

1. Remember that written 8th notes are performed as swung 8th notes. For more information regarding the interpretation of swing 8th notes, see Chapter 2 of *Jazz Theory—From Basic to Advanced Study*.

Appendix B
Common-Practice Harmony at the Keyboard

MASTER THE FUNDAMENTALS

UNIT 1   Triads in Root Position and Inversions[1]

Lead-Sheet Notation[2]—Keyboard Texture

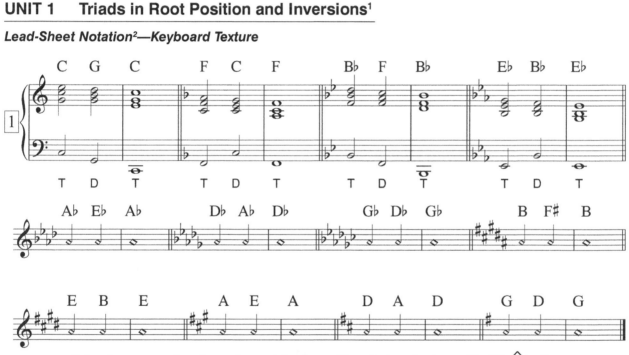

Exercise 1.1.1 **A tonic expansion in major and minor.** Play 3x beginning with (1) $\hat{1}$ in the soprano; (2) $\hat{3}$ in the soprano; and (3) $\hat{5}$ in the soprano.[3]

Exercise 1.1.1 continued

Exercise 1.1.2 The Romanesca.[4] Transpose to G, F, and A.

Exercise 1.1.3 Realize in keyboard texture. Play 3x beginning with (1) $\hat{1}$ in the soprano; (2) $\hat{3}$ in the soprano; and (3) $\hat{5}$ in the soprano. Transpose to two keys.

Roman Numerals[5]—Keyboard Texture

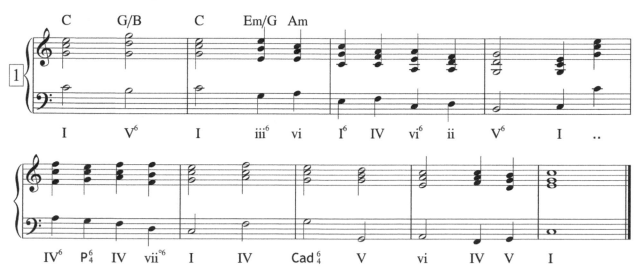

Exercise 1.2 Realize in keyboard texture. Transpose to two keys and analyze with chord symbols using lead-sheet notation.[6]

Exercise 1.2 continued

Figured-Bass Notation—Keyboard Texture[7]

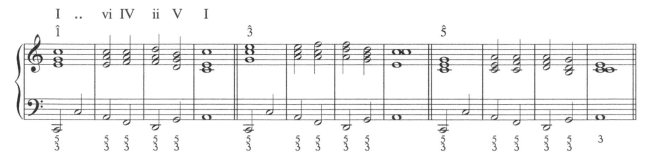

Exercise 1.3.1 **A tonic expansion in three positions.** Transpose to G, D, A, F, B♭, and E♭.

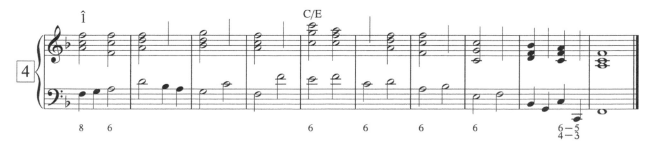

Exercise 1.3.2 **Provide the missing chords.** Transpose to two keys and analyze with chord symbols using lead-sheet notation.

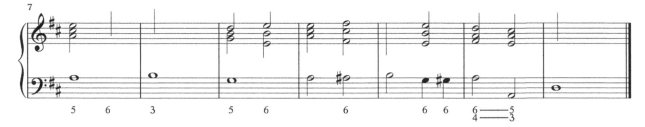

Exercise 1.3.2 continued

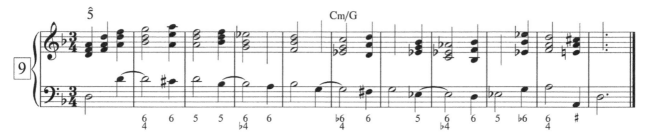

Exercise 1.3.2 continued

Exercise 1.3.3 Tonic expansions in major and minor. Play each progression 3x beginning with (1) $\hat{1}$ in the soprano; (2) $\hat{3}$ in the soprano; and (3) $\hat{5}$ in the soprano.

Exercise 1.3.3 continued

Exercise 1.3.4 **Realize in keyboard texture.** Transpose to two keys and analyze with chord symbols using lead-sheet notation.

UNIT 2   Four-Part Chords in Root Position (7)

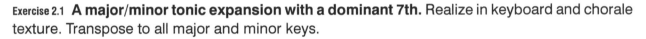

Exercise 2.1 A major/minor tonic expansion with a dominant 7th. Realize in keyboard and chorale texture. Transpose to all major and minor keys.

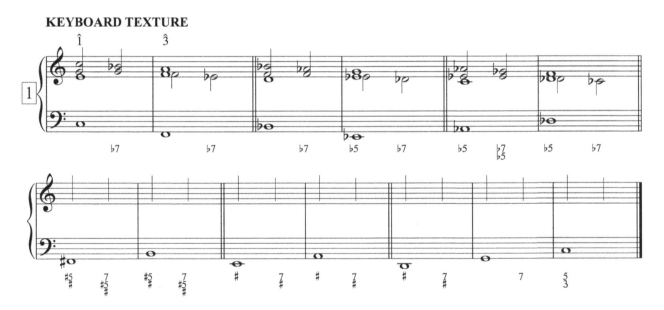

Exercise 2.2 A descending cycle of dominant 7ths. Compare the harmonic progressions realized in keyboard and chorale texture. Play each progression 3x beginning with (1) 1̂ in the soprano; (2) 3̂ in the soprano; and (3) 5̂ in the soprano. Provide the missing chords.

CHORALE TEXTURE

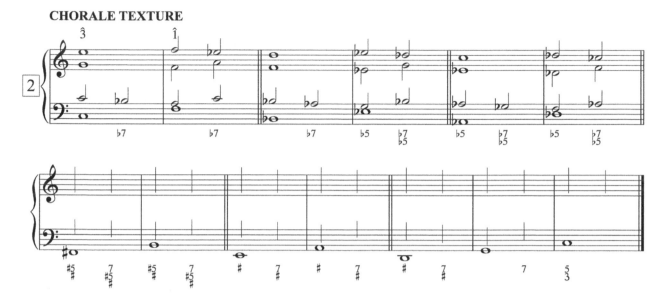

Exercise 2.2 continued

KEYBOARD TEXTURE

CHORALE TEXTURE

Exercise 2.3 An ascending cycle of dominant 7ths. Compare the harmonic progressions realized in keyboard and chorale texture. Transpose to G, D, F, and B♭. Provide a harmonic analysis using lead-sheet symbols.

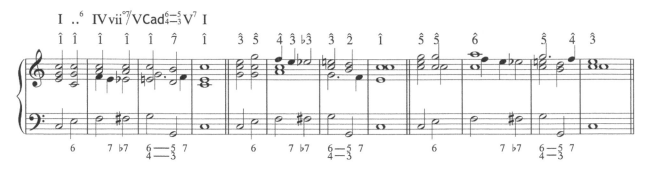

Exercise 2.4 A diminished 7th cadential preparation in major. Transpose to G, D, F, and B♭.

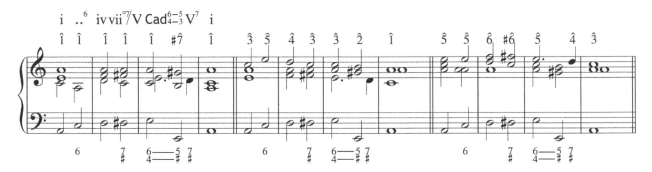

Exercise 2.5 A diminished 7th cadential preparation in minor. Transpose to Dm, Gm, Cm, Em, Bm, and F♯m.

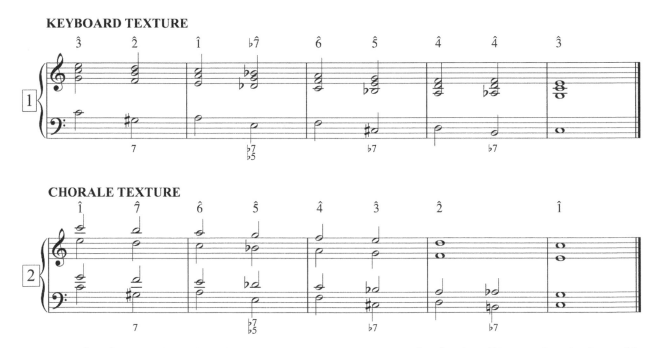

Exercise 2.6 A minor 3rd cycle with lower chromatic diminished 7ths. Play 3x beginning with (1) $\hat{1}$ in the soprano; (2) $\hat{3}$ in the soprano; and (3) $\hat{5}$ in the soprano. Compare the harmonic progressions realized in keyboard and chorale texture. Transpose to D, A, B♭, and E♭. Provide a harmonic analysis using lead-sheet symbols.

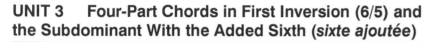

Exercise 2.7 Realize in keyboard and chorale texture. Transpose to two keys and provide a contextual analysis using Roman numerals.

UNIT 3   Four-Part Chords in First Inversion (6/5) and the Subdominant With the Added Sixth (*sixte ajoutée*)

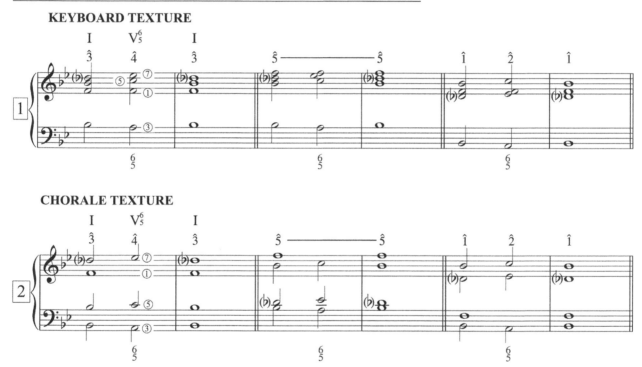

Exercise 3.1 A major/minor tonic expansion with 6/5 chords in all positions. Realize in keyboard and chorale texture. Transpose to all major and minor keys.

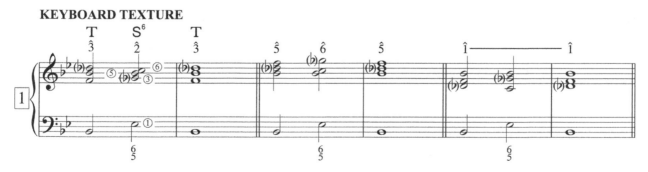

Exercise 3.2 The subdominant with the added sixth (*sixte ajoutée*) in all positions. Realize in keyboard and chorale texture. Transpose to all major and minor keys.

CHORALE TEXTURE

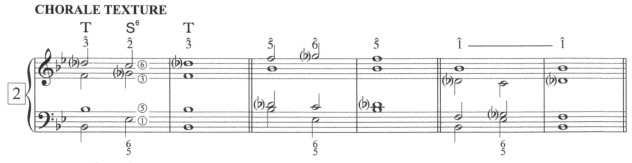

Exercise 3.2 continued

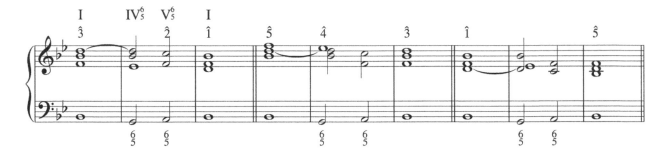

Exercise 3.3 Successive 6/5 chords in major. Transpose to all major keys.

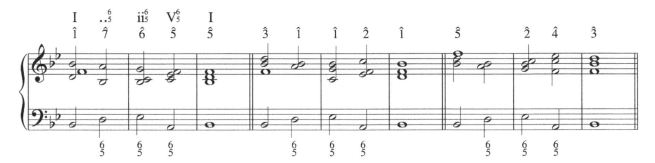

Exercise 3.4 Multiple 6/5 chords. Transpose to all major keys.

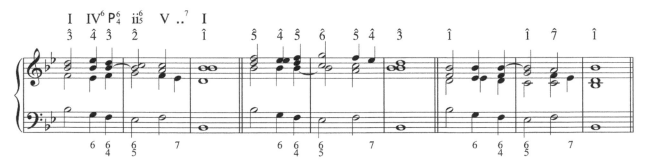

Exercise 3.5 A passing 6/4 chord between IV⁶—IV in all positions. Transpose to all major keys.

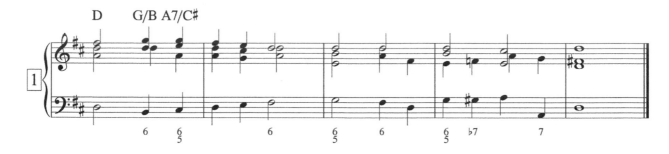

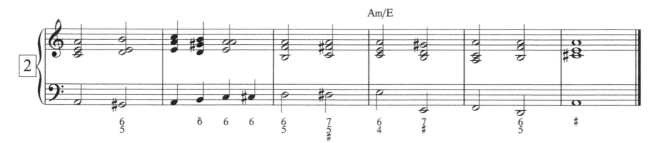

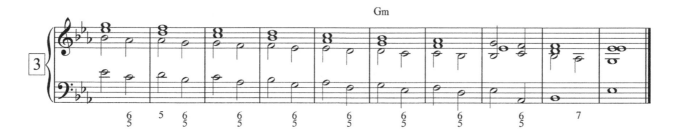

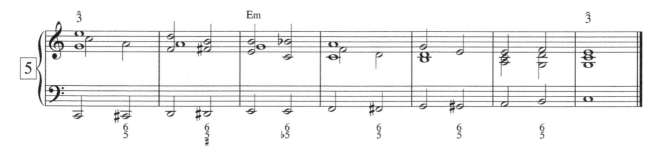

Exercise 3.6 6/5 chords in different harmonic contexts. Transpose to three keys and provide a harmonic analysis using lead-sheet symbols.

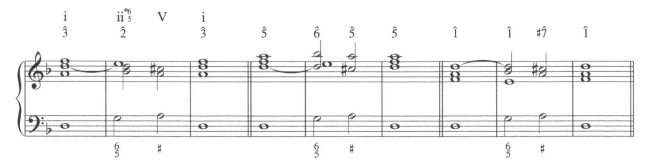

Exercise 3.7 The 6/5 chord as a dominant preparation in minor. Transpose to all minor keys.

Exercise 3.8 Successive 6/5 chords in minor. Transpose to all minor keys.

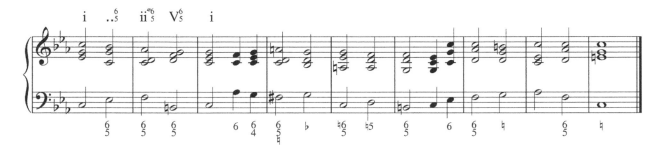

Exercise 3.9 Multiple 6/5 chords. Transpose to three keys and provide a contextual analysis using Roman numerals.

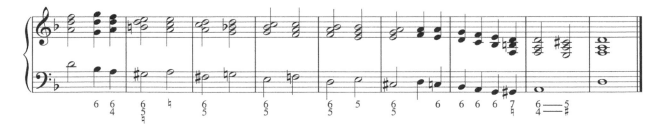

Exercise 3.10 A passing 6/4 and parallel 6th chords. Transpose to all major keys.

Exercise 3.11 **Realize in keyboard style.** Realize the following progressions, transpose to three keys, and provide a contextual analysis using Roman numerals.

UNIT 4   Four-Part Chords in Second (6/4/3) and Third Inversion (6/4/2)

KEYBOARD TEXTURE

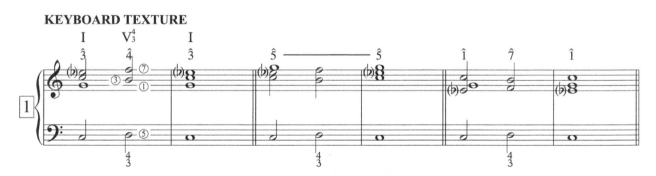

Exercise 4.1 **A major/minor tonic expansion with a 6/4/3 chord.** Realize in keyboard and chorale texture. Transpose to all major and minor keys.

CHORALE TEXTURE

Exercise 4.1 continued

Exercise 4.2 A descending octave with 6/4/3 chords. Transpose to G, D, A, and E.

KEYBOARD TEXTURE

CHORALE TEXTURE

Exercise 4.3 Chromatic passing 6/4/3 chords. Compare the harmonic progressions realized in keyboard and chorale texture. Transpose to C, G, D, and B♭. Provide a harmonic analysis using lead-sheet symbols.

KEYBOARD TEXTURE

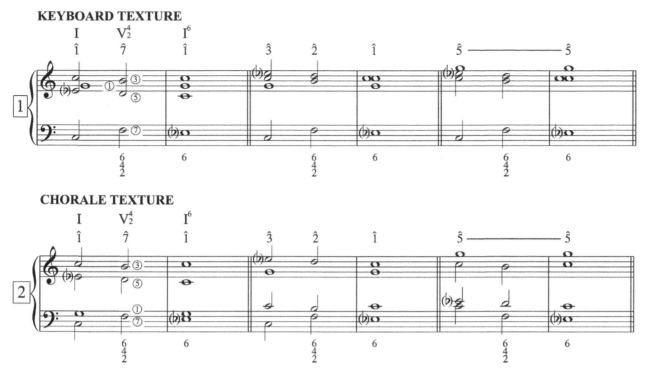

CHORALE TEXTURE

Exercise 4.4 A major/minor tonic expansion with a 6/4/2 chord. Realize in keyboard and chorale texture. Transpose to all major and minor keys.

KEYBOARD TEXTURE

CHORALE TEXTURE

Exercise 4.5 Descending chromatic scale with 6/4/2 chords. Compare the harmonic progressions realized in keyboard and chorale texture. Transpose to three keys.

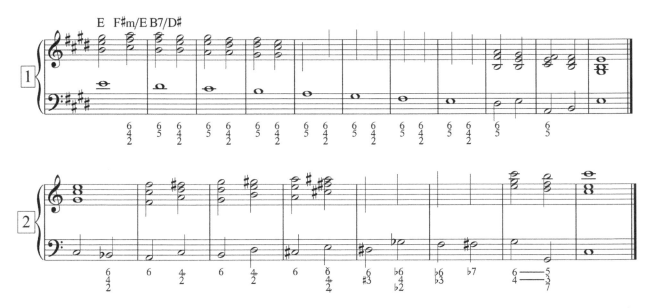

Exercise 4.6 **6/4/2 chords in different harmonic contexts.** Transpose to three keys.

Exercise 4.7 **Fill in the missing chords.** Transpose to three keys. Provide a harmonic analysis using lead-sheet symbols.

Exercise 4.7 continued

UNIT 5   Figured-Bass Exercises

Exercise 5.1 **A journey through all keys.** Play 3x beginning with (1) a chordal root in the soprano; (2) a 3rd in the soprano; and (3) a 5th in the soprano.

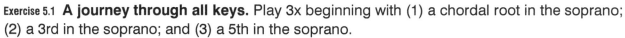

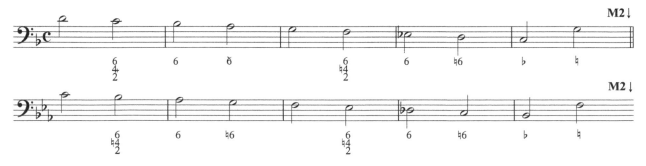

Exercise 5.2 **A journey through all keys.** Continue the progression down a major 2nd.

Exercise 5.3 **Realize in keyboard texture.** Transpose to two keys and provide a contextual analysis using Roman numerals.

UNIT 6   The 4–3 Suspension

The 4–3 suspension occurs in different voices except the bass voice. Possible use: (1) chords moving by ascending 5ths (descending 4ths): I—V, I⁶—V, ii—vi, etc.; or (2) chords moving by ascending 2nds: V—vi, etc.

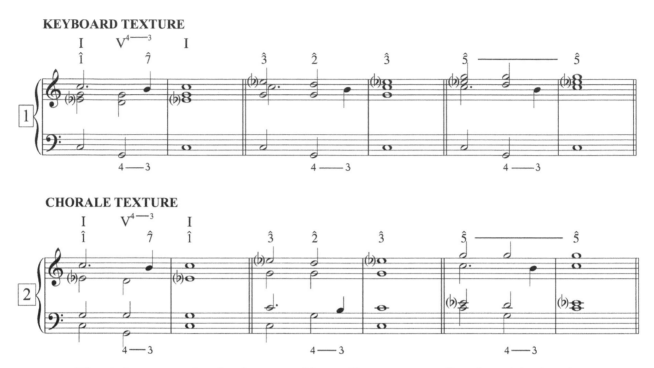

Exercise 6.1 **The 4–3 suspension in three positions.** Transpose to all major and minor keys.

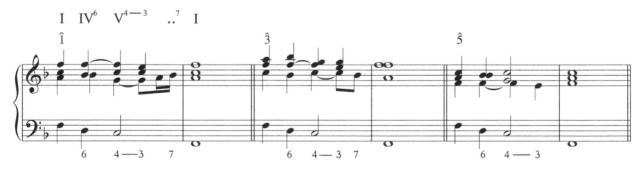

Exercise 6.2 **The 4–3 suspension in three positions in major.** Transpose to G, D, and B♭.

Exercise 6.3 **The 4–3 suspension in three positions in minor.** Transpose to Gm, Em, and Bm.

Exercise 6.4 **The 4–3 suspension in three positions in major.** Transpose to G, F, and B♭.

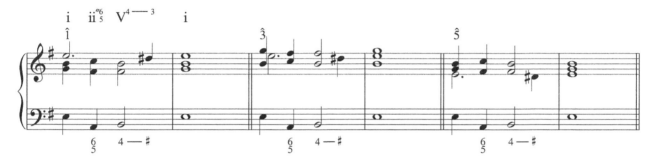

Exercise 6.5 **The 4–3 suspension in three positions in minor.** Transpose to Dm, Gm, and Bm.

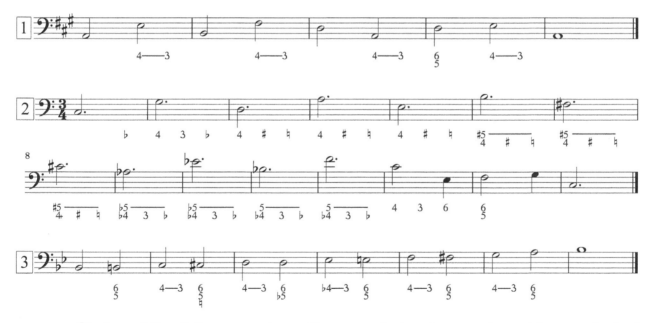

Exercise 6.6 **Chains of the 4–3 suspensions.** Transpose to two keys and provide a contextual analysis using Roman numerals.

UNIT 7   The 9–8 Suspension

The 9–8 suspension occurs in different voices except the bass voice. Possible use: (1) chords moving by descending 5ths (ascending 4ths): I—IV, I⁶—IV, ii—V, etc.; or (2) chords moving by ascending 2nds: V—vi, etc.

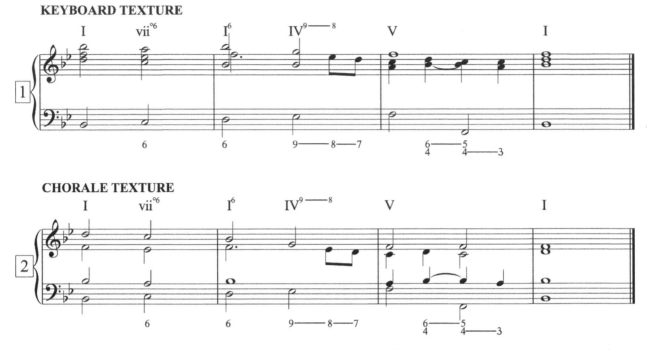

Exercise 7.1 The 9–8 suspension in a I⁶—IV progression. Compare the harmonic progressions realized in keyboard and chorale texture. Transpose to C, G, D, A, E, F, E♭, and A♭.

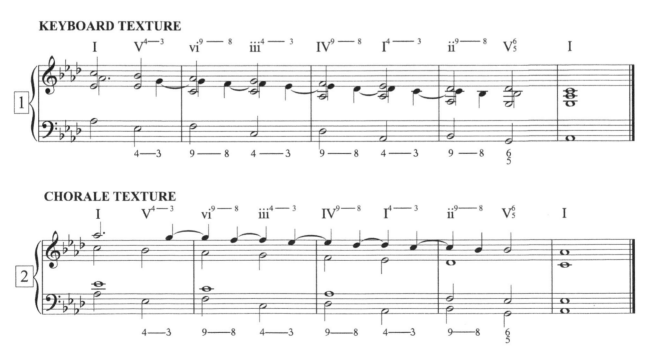

Exercise 7.2 The 4–3 and 9–8 suspensions. Compare the harmonic progressions realized in keyboard and chorale texture. Transpose to C, G, D, A, E, F, B♭, and E♭.

Exercise 7.3 **Realize in keyboard texture.** Transpose to three keys and provide a contextual analysis using Roman numerals.

UNIT 8   The 7–6 Suspension

The 7–6 suspension occurs in different voices except the bass voice. It appears in chord successions wherein the second chord is in first inversion. Possible use: (1) chords moving by ascending 2nds: I—viiᵒ⁶, etc.; or (2) chords moving by descending 2nds: iii⁶—ii⁶, etc.

KEYBOARD TEXTURE

Exercise 8.1 **The 7–6 suspension in three positions.** Compare the harmonic progressions realized in keyboard and chorale texture. Transpose to all major and minor keys.

CHORALE TEXTURE

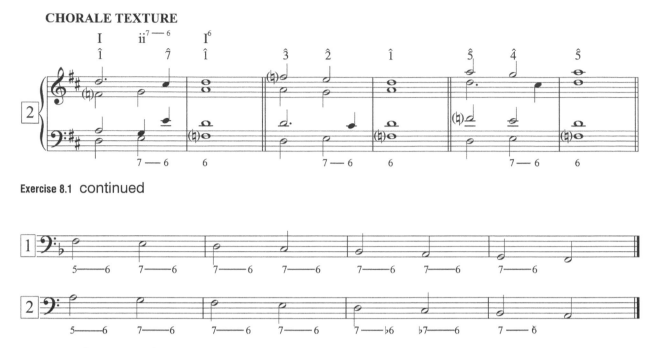

Exercise 8.1 continued

Exercise 8.2 A descending chain of 7–6 suspensions. Transpose to three keys and provide a contextual analysis using Roman numerals.

UNIT 9   The 2–3 Bass Suspension

The 2–3 bass suspension occurs only in the bass voice. Possible use: chords moving by ascending 5ths (descending 4ths), in which the second chord is in first inversion: I—V⁶, IV—I⁶, vi—iii⁶, etc.

KEYBOARD TEXTURE

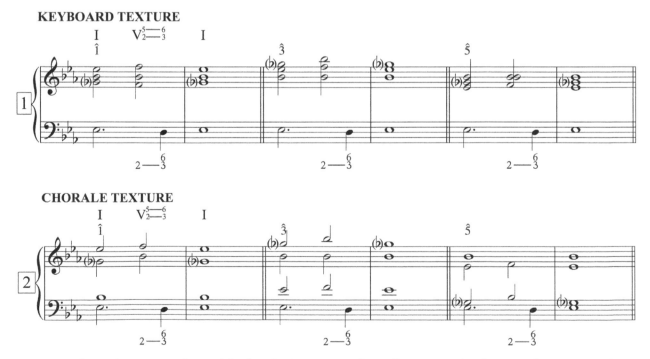

CHORALE TEXTURE

Exercise 9.1 A tonic expansion with the 2–3 suspension. Compare the harmonic progressions realized in keyboard and chorale texture. Transpose to all major and minor keys.

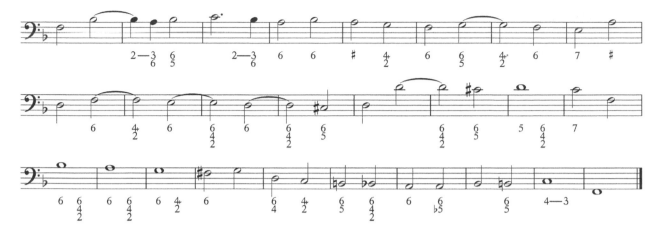

Exercise 9.2 **Realize in keyboard texture.** Transpose to D and provide a harmonic analysis using Roman numerals.

UNIT 10   Double and Triple Suspensions and Melodic Retardations

Exercise 10.1 **Combinations of suspensions in major.** Transpose to two keys and provide a harmonic analysis using Roman numerals.

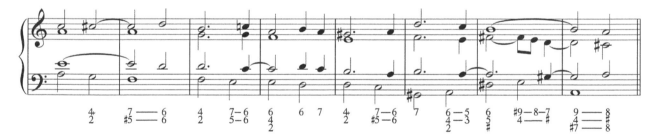

Exercise 10.2 **Combinations of suspensions in minor.** Transpose to two keys and provide a harmonic analysis using Roman numerals.

FUNDAMENTALS TO MASTERY

UNIT 11   Figured-Bass Progressions With Suspensions

Exercise 11.1 **Realize in keyboard texture.** Transpose to two keys and provide a harmonic analysis using Roman numerals.

Exercise 11.1 continued

Koechlin

Exercise 11.1 continued

UNIT 12   Cadential Gestures

Transpose to all major and minor keys.

Authentic Cadence (cadenza semplice)

Authentic cadences contain at least two chords: V (dominant) and I (tonic). Based on the degree of melodic closure, they can occur in the perfect form (when the soprano ends on $\hat{1}$ and the bass leaps from $\hat{5}$ to $\hat{1}$) or the imperfect form (when the soprano closes on $\hat{3}$ or $\hat{5}$ while the bass leaps from $\hat{5}$ to $\hat{1}$).

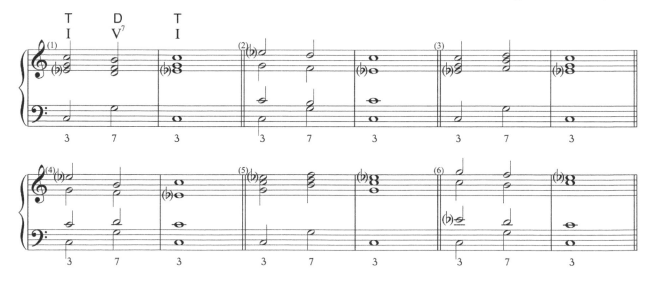

Expanded Authentic Cadence (cadenza doppia)

An expanded authentic cadence features a predominant chord that can take the forms of (1) IV; (2) ii; (3) ii⁶; or (4) ii⁶₅ (with contextual tonal modifications reflecting major and/or minor keys).

Authentic Cadences With Suspensions (cadenze lunghe)

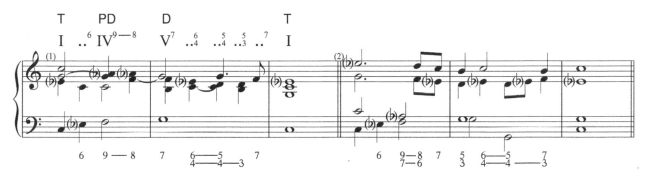

Expanded Authentic Cadences With Suspensions

Plagal Cadences (church cadences)

Plagal cadences contain two harmonic formations: I (tonic) and IV (subdominant). The IV chord often contains an added 6th, which resolves up a second onto the third of a tonic chord. Even though the subdominant with an added 6th has the same pitches as the predominant chord on $\hat{2}$ (ii$_5^6$), they have a completely different functional behavior and distribution of chordal dissonances. Based on the stylistic conventions of a given musical period, the subdominant chord can occur in many pitch configurations and harmonic guises.

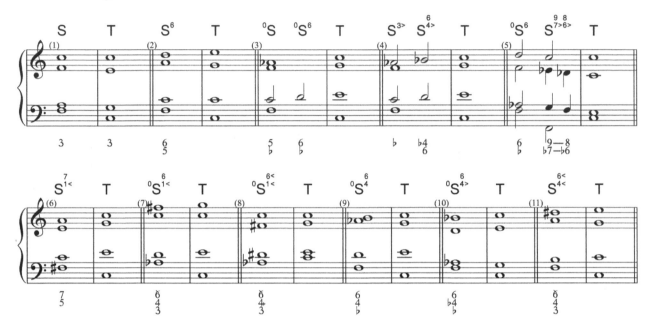

Characteristic Cadences

A Neapolitan Cadence

A Neapolitan cadence usually occurs in minor keys and contains the Neapolitan-sixth chord (N^6), which is a major triad in first inversion built on $\hat{4}$. The root of the Neapolitan-sixth chord occurs on $\flat\hat{2}$, giving it strong Phrygian connotations ($\flat\hat{2}$–$\hat{1}$). To facilitate a correct voice-leading treatment, the "root" ($\hat{4}$) of the Neapolitan-sixth chord is doubled.

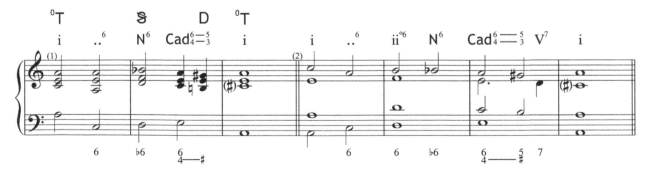

A Bachian Cadence

A Bachian cadence is the harmonic variant of a Neapolitan cadence and contains a diminished passing chord built on $\sharp\hat{4}$, linking the Neapolitan-sixth chord with a dominant on $\hat{5}$.

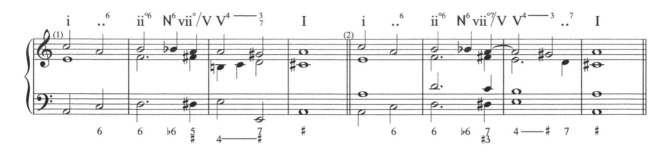

Half Cadences (demi-cadence; Halbschluss)

Half cadences end inconclusively on a dominant chord.

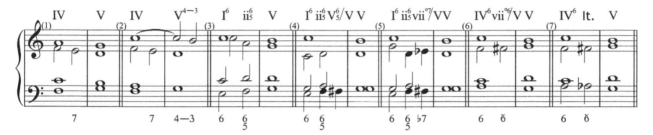

A Phrygian Cadence

A Phrygian cadence is the characteristic variant of a half cadence in which the bass voice features a "Phrygian" half-step descend (♭)$\hat{6}$–$\hat{5}$ while the soprano ascends from $\hat{4}$ to $\hat{5}$, connecting iv⁶ with V.

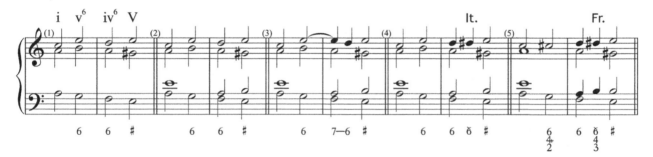

Deceptive Cadences (cadence rompue; Trugschluss; cadenza finta)

Deceptive cadences postpone the arrival of a root-position tonic chord.

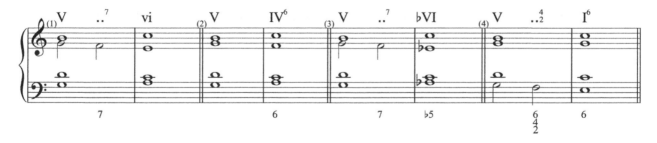

Techniques of Evading Cadences[8] (cadence évité)

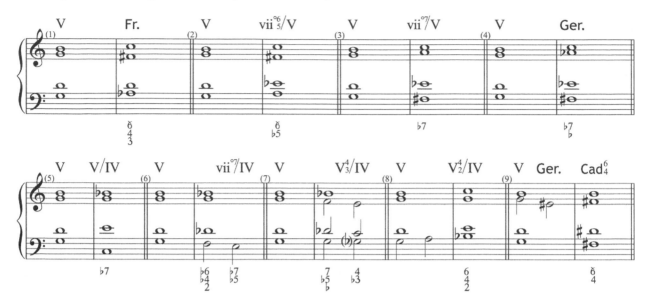

Harmonic Progressions With Augmented 6th Chords

The augmented 6th chords are chromatic formations built on $\flat\hat{6}$ that anticipate the arrival of a dominant sonority (or its acceptable variants) through a contrapuntal/chromatic convergence from above ($\flat\hat{6}-\hat{5}$) and below ($\sharp\hat{4}-\hat{5}$) in contrary motion. They typically come in three national flavors—Italian, German, and French—and, because their pitch structure closely resembles that of a dominant 7th chord, they can function as effective modulatory devices.

The Italian chord (It.)—it resembles an enharmonic dominant 7th chord without the fifth.[9]

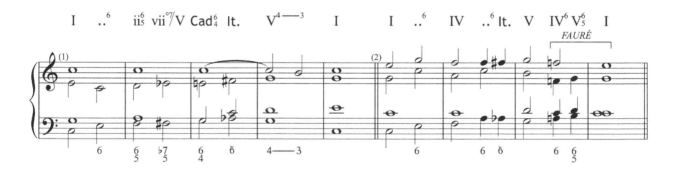

The German chord (Ger.)—it resembles an enharmonic dominant 7th chord, which resolves onto a 6/4 chord (passing or cadential).

The French chord (Fr.)—it resembles an enharmonic dominant 7th chord with a lowered fifth.

A Chopin Cadence

A Chopin cadence contains the Chopin chord, which is a dominant 7th with an added 13th. For the best sonic effect, the 13th should be placed in the soprano voice.

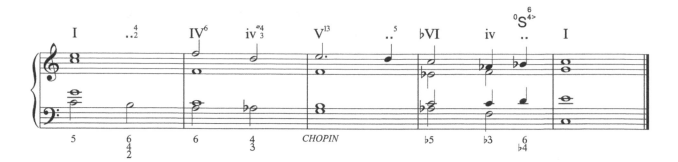

A Tristan Cadence

A Tristan cadence appears at the opening of Richard Wagner's opera *Tristan and Isolde* and contains an enharmonic half-diminished 7th chord (ø7) built on (♭)$\hat{6}$, which resolves onto an altered dominant 7th.[10]

UNIT 13   The Rule of the Octave (*la règle de l'octave*[11])—Historical Realizations

Transpose the following settings of the Rule of the Octave to all keys.

"Modal" Rules of the Octave

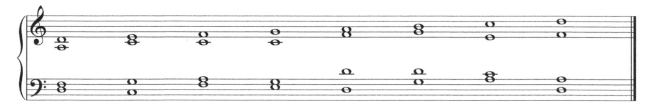

Mode 1—*Dorian* (I. protos autentus)

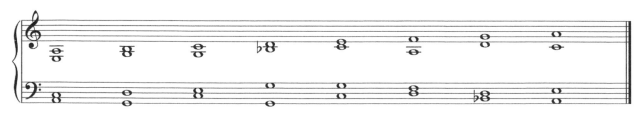

Mode 2—*Hypodorian* (II. protos plagalis)

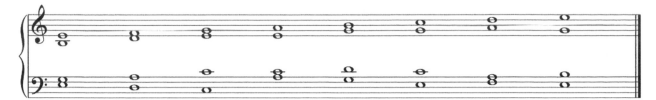

Mode 3—*Phrygian* (III. deuteros autentus)

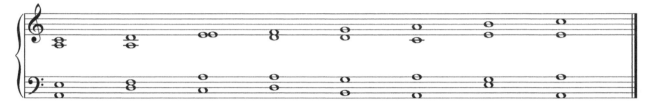

Mode 4—*Hypophrygian* (IV. deuteros plagalis)

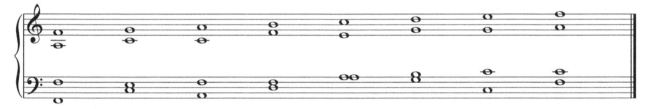

Mode 5—*Lydian* (V. tritos autentus)

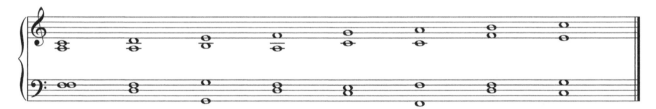

Mode 6—*Hypolydian* (VI. tritos plagalis)

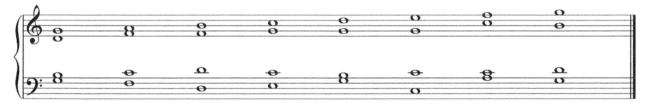

Mode 7—*Mixolydian* (VII. tetrardos autentus)

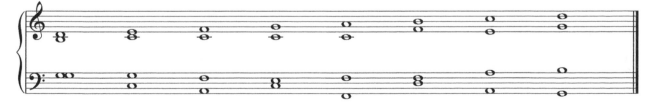

Mode 8—*Hypomixolydian* (VIII. tetrardos plagalis)

Tomás de Sancta Maria, *Arte de tañer fantasia (1565)*[12]

Girolamo Diruta, *Il Transilvano* (1609)[13]

Spiridionis a Monte Carmelo, *Nova Instruction* (1670)[14]

Francesco Gasparini, *L'armonico pratico al cimbalo* (1708)

Francesco Gasparini, *L'armonico pratico al cimbalo* (1708)

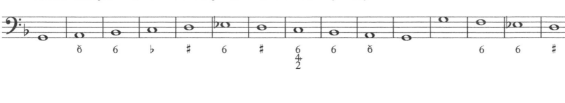

François Campion, *Traité d'Accompagnement et de Composition selon la règle des octaves de musique (1716)*

Johann David Heinichen, *Der General-Baß in der Composition* (1728)

Major   Minor

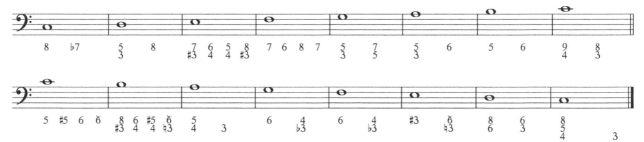

Nicola Porpora, *Partimenti* (ca. 1755)[15]

C.P.E. Bach, *Versuch über die wahre Art das Clavier zu spielen* (1762)

C.P.E. Bach, *Versuch über die wahre Art das Clavier zu spielen* (1762)

C.P.E. Bach, *Versuch über die wahre Art das Clavier zu spielen* (1762)

Fedele Fenaroli, *Regola musical per i principianti di cembolo* (1775)

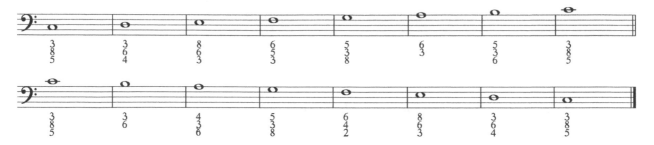

Giacomo Tritto, *Partimenti e Regole generali* (1821)

François-Joseph Fétis, *Traité complet de la théorie et de la practique de l'harmonie* (1844)

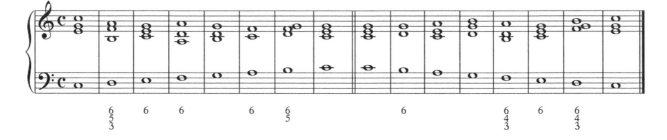

François-Auguste Gaveart, *Traité d'harmonie théorique at practique* (1907)—Diatonic Rule of the Octave

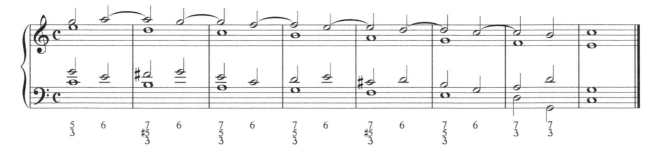

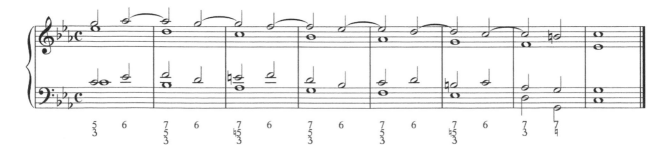

François-Auguste Gaveart, *Traité d'harmonie théorique at practique* (1907)—Chromatic Rule of the Octave

UNIT 14   Sequential Progressions Derived From the Rule of the Octave

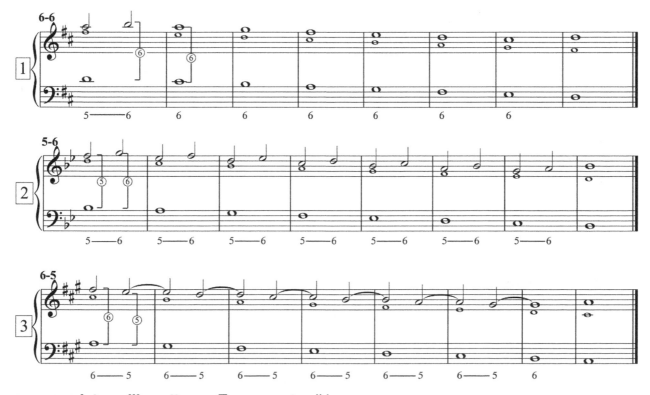

Exercise 14.1 **Intervallic patterns.** Transpose to all keys.

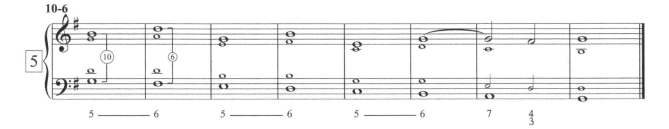

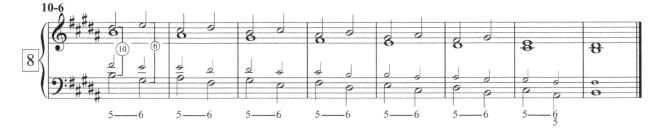

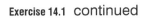

Exercise 14.1 continued

UNIT 15   The Lament Bass

The lament bass contains a diatonic tetrachord $\hat{8}$–$\hat{7}$–$\hat{6}$–$\hat{5}$ or its chromaticized version $\hat{8}$–$\hat{7}$–♭$\hat{7}$–$\hat{6}$–♭$\hat{6}$–$\hat{5}$. Historically, the lament bass provided a structural foundation for various improvisatory genres, such as chaconne (ciaconna) and passacaglia.[16]

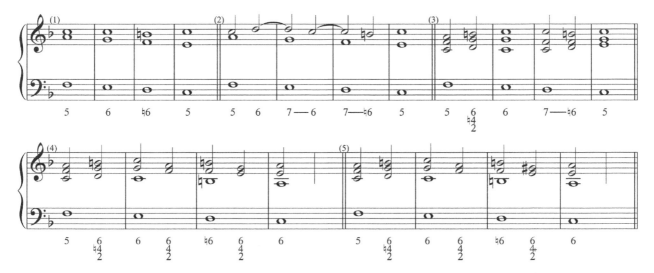

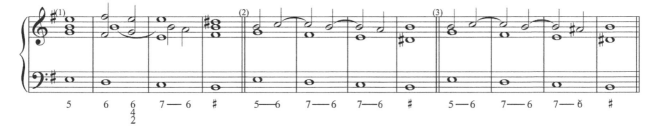

Exercise 15.1 Diatonic tetrachord in major (chaconne). Transpose to C, G, and B♭.

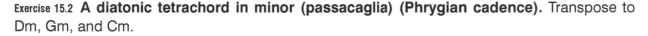

Exercise 15.2 A diatonic tetrachord in minor (passacaglia) (Phrygian cadence). Transpose to Dm, Gm, and Cm.

Exercise 15.3 A chromatic tetrachord (*passus duriusculus*). Transpose to Am, Dm, and Gm.

UNIT 16 Harmonic Progressions With *Basso Ostinato*

Besides the chaconne and the passacaglia, which are the most important *basso ostinato* formulas, there are other ground bass progressions, including the *passamezzo antico*, the *passamezzo moderno*, the *la folia*, the *bergamasca*, and the *romanesca*, that occur in many harmonic, melodic, and rhythmic guises.

Transpose to two keys.

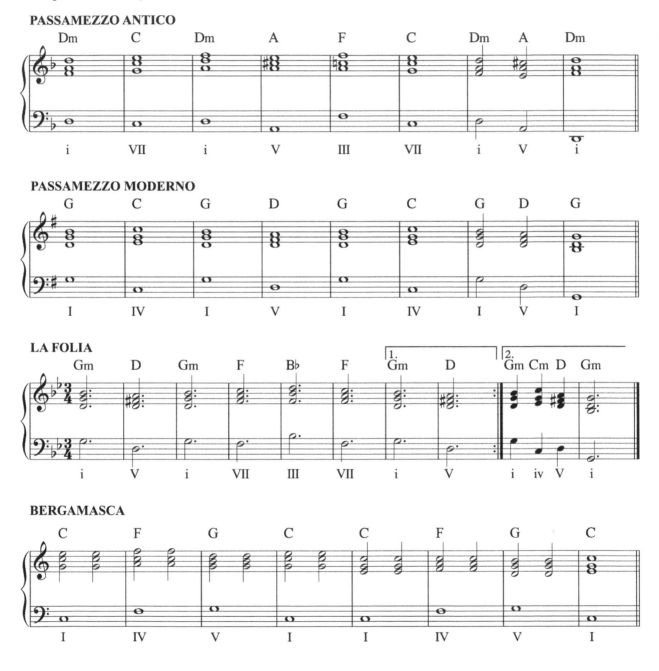

ROMANESCA   **VARIATION 1**

VARIATION 2   **VARIATION 3**

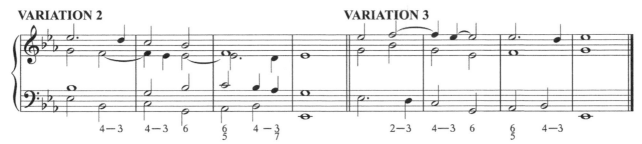

PASSACAGLIA

UNIT 17   Galant Style—Harmonic Schematas

Galant schematas constitute characteristic harmonic progressions, melodic devices, and/or contrapuntal frameworks that are extremely helpful in acquiring improvisational and compositional skills.[17]

Transpose to two keys.

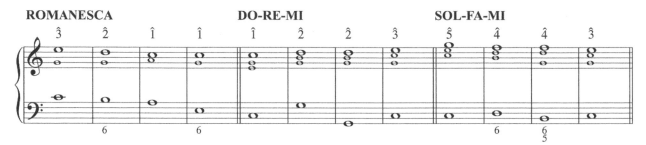

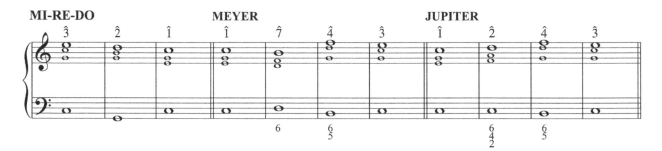

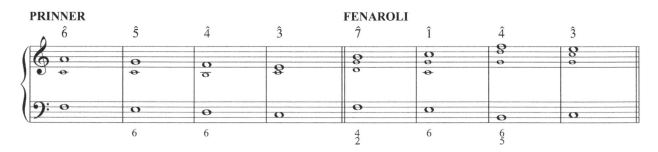

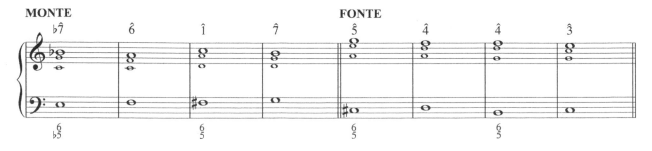

UNIT 18   Partimenti[18]

Handel

Exercise 18.1 Realize in keyboard texture. Transpose to two keys and provide a harmonic analysis using Roman numerals.

Exercise 18.1 continued

Exercise 18.1 continued

Exercise 18.1 continued

Exercise 18.1 continued

Handel

Handel

Exercise 18.1 continued

MASTERY TO EXCELLENCE

UNIT 19   Partimenti—Unfigured Bass

Exercise 19.1 **Realize in keyboard texture.** Transpose to two keys and provide a harmonic analysis using Roman numerals.

Exercise 19.1 continued

UNIT 20 Chromaticism

Exercise 20.1 Harmonic applications of the *Tristan* chord. Continue according to the specified intervallic pattern.

Exercise 20.1 continued

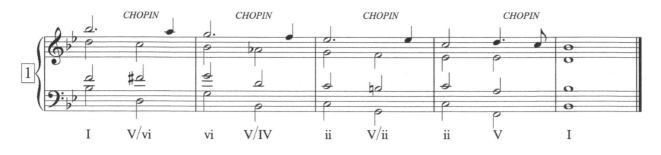

I   V/vi   vi   V/IV   ii   V/ii   ii   V   I

I V/vi IV vii°⁷/ii ii V/ii ♭VII vii°⁷/v v V/v ♭III vii°⁷/i i V ♭VI iv I

Exercise 20.2 **Harmonic applications of the *Chopin* chord.** Transpose to F, G, and D.

The Omnibus Progression[19] *(OMN)*

KEYBOARD TEXTURE

CHORALE TEXTURE

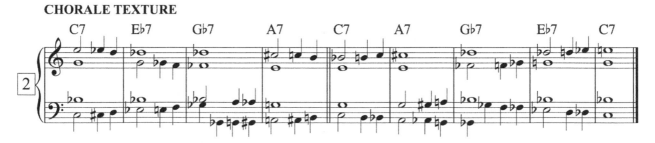

Exercise 20.3 **The Omnibus progression.** Play 3x beginning with (1) a chordal root in the soprano; (2) a 3rd in the soprano; and (3) a 7th in the soprano. Begin on D♭7 and D7. Compare the harmonic progressions realized in keyboard and chorale texture.

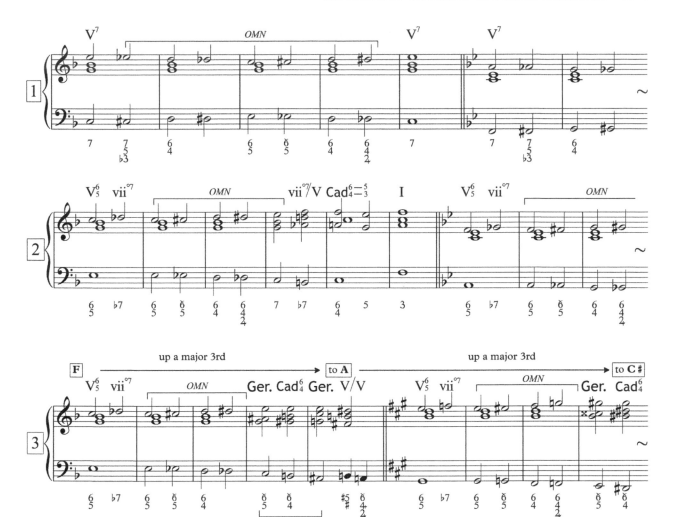

Exercise 20.4 The Omnibus progression as a dominant expansion. Continue through all keys.

The Omnibus With a Chromatic Plagal Cadence

Exercise 20.5 Harmonic transformations of the Omnibus. Start each progression on D♭ and D.[20]

The Omnibus With Inverted Half-Diminished 7th Chords

The Omnibus With Inverted Dominant 7th Chords

Exercise 20.5 continued

The Omnibus With Altered Dominant 7ths, Half-Diminished 7ths, and Augmented Triads

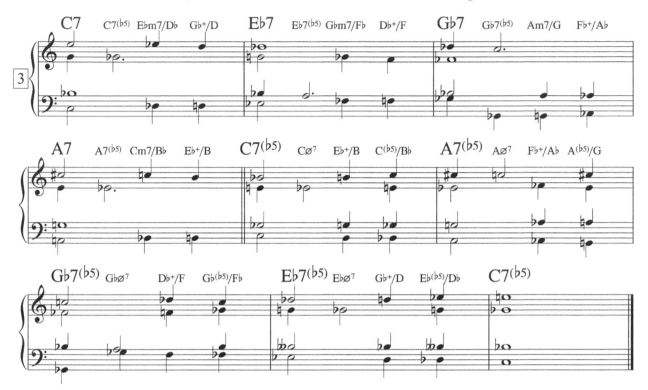

Exercise 20.5 continued

Exercise 20.6 Diminished 7th chords. Continue through all keys.

Exercise 20.7 Cyclic progressions with an augmented triad. Continue according to the specified intervallic pattern.

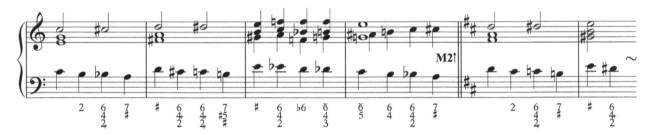

Exercise 20.8 Modified Omnibus with the French chord. Continue according to the specified intervallic pattern.

Exercise 20.9 Dominant pedal points. Continue according to the specified intervallic pattern.

Exercise 20.9 continued

The B-A-C-H motive is a musical signature of J. S. Bach and contains four pitches: (1) B♭ (**B**); (2) **A**; (3) **C** i; (4) B (**H**). That musical signature was frequently adopted as a subject of various musical compositions by Robert Schumann, Franz Liszt, Max Reger, and many others.

Exercise 20.10 **The B-A-C-H motive.** Continue through all keys.

Exercise 20.10 continued

Exercise 20.11 **Whole-tone progressions with chromatic formations.** Start each progression a half step higher.

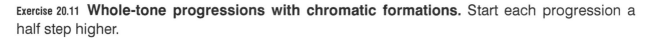

Exercise 20.12 **Whole-tone progression in minor.** Transpose to two keys.

G#+ A⁹⁽♭⁵⁾ B♭+ B⁹⁽♭⁵⁾   C+ C♯⁹⁽♭⁵⁾ D+ E♭⁹⁽♭⁵⁾   E+ F⁹⁽♭⁵⁾ F♯+ G⁹⁽♭⁵⁾   G♯+

Exercise 20.13 Chromatic wedge (stable)—augmented triads and altered dominant 9ths. Transpose to three keys.

F♯⁹⁽♭⁵⁾ G+ A♭⁹⁽♭⁵⁾ A+   B♭⁹⁽♭⁵⁾ B+ C⁹⁽♭⁵⁾ C♯+   D⁹⁽♭⁵⁾ E♭+ E⁹⁽♭⁵⁾ F+   F♯⁹⁽♭⁵⁾

Exercise 20.14 Chromatic wedge (less stable)—augmented triads and altered dominant 9ths. Transpose to three keys.

Am⁽△⁷⁾ B♭¹³⁽♭⁹⁾sus Bm⁽△⁷⁾ C¹³⁽♭⁹⁾sus D♭m⁽△⁷⁾ D¹³⁽♭⁹⁾sus E♭m⁽△⁷⁾ E¹³⁽♭⁹⁾sus Fm⁽△⁷⁾ F♯¹³⁽♭⁹⁾sus Gm⁽△⁷⁾ G♯¹³⁽♭⁹⁾sus Am⁽△⁷⁾

Exercise 20.15 Chromatic wedge (unstable)—minor–major 7th and altered dominant 7ths. Transpose to three keys.

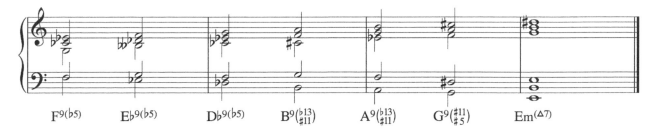

F⁹⁽♭⁵⁾   E♭⁹⁽♭⁵⁾   D♭⁹⁽♭⁵⁾   B⁹⁽♭¹³ ♯¹¹⁾   A⁹⁽♭¹³ ♯¹¹⁾   G⁹⁽♯¹¹ ♯⁵⁾   Em⁽△⁷⁾

Exercise 20.16 Whole-tone chromatic wedge and parallel augmented triads. Transpose to two keys.

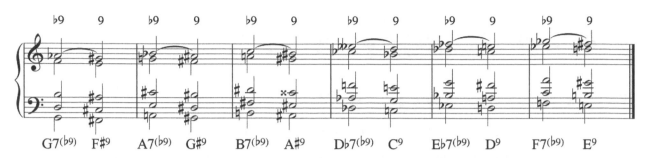

Exercise 20.17 Common-tone retention between extended dominant formations. Continue through all keys.

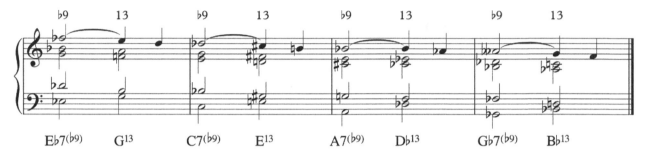

Exercise 20.18 Common-tone retention between extended dominant formations. Transpose the progression up a minor 2nd.

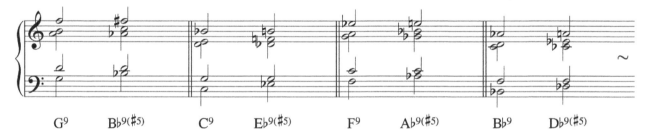

Exercise 20.19 Semitone voice leading between extended dominant formations. Continue through all keys.

UNIT 21 Melody Harmonization

Melodic Patterns

Exercises 21.1–21.5 contain several melodic patterns frequently found in chorale melodies. These patterns have been realized in different ways and offer multiple harmonic choices for the realization of chorales. Realize all the patterns in keyboard (1 + 3) and chorale (2 + 2) texture.

Exercise 21.1 **The $\hat{3}$–$\hat{2}$–$\hat{1}$ melodic pattern.** Transpose to four major and minor keys.

Exercise 21.2 **The $\hat{4}$–$\hat{3}$–$\hat{2}$–$\hat{1}$ melodic pattern.** Transpose to four major and minor keys.

Exercise 21.2 continued

Exercise 21.3 The $\hat{1}$–$\hat{2}$–$\hat{3}$ **melodic pattern.** Transpose to four major and minor keys.

Exercise 21.4 The $\hat{4}$– $\hat{3}$– $\hat{2}$ **melodic pattern.** Transpose to four major and minor keys.

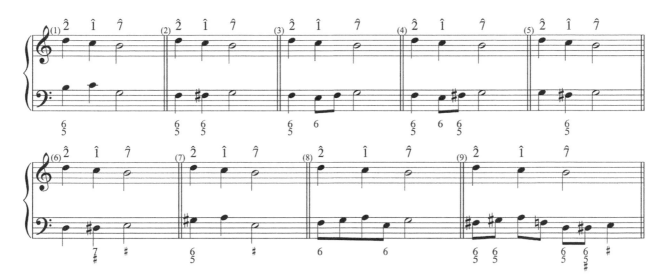

Exercise 21.5 The $\hat{2}$– $\hat{1}$– $\hat{7}$ **melodic pattern.** Transpose to four major and minor keys.

Exercise 21.6 **Théodore Dubois's realizations of the** $\hat{1}$– $\hat{7}$– $\hat{1}$ **melodic pattern.**[21] Transpose to three keys.

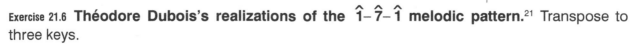

Exercise 21.6 Théodore Dubois's realizations of the $\hat{1}$–$\hat{7}$–$\hat{1}$ melodic pattern.[21] Transpose to three keys.

Exercise 21.6 continued

Vater unser im Himmelreich

Nun komm, der Heiden Heiland

Jesu, der du meine Seele

Exercise 21.7 Chorales. Provide two different chorale-style realizations (one diatonic and one chromatic) for each of the following chorale melodies. Use some of the harmonic ideas from Exercises 21.1–21.5.

Exercise 21.8 Basic melodies for harmonization. Provide two different chorale-style realizations for each of the following melodies.

Grieg

Exercise 21.8 continued

Arensky

Louis/Thuille

Exercise 21.9 Intermediate melodies for harmonization. Provide two different chorale-style realizations for each of the following melodies.

Challan

Kholopov

Sposobin

Exercise 21.9 continued

Exercise 21.10 Advanced melodies for harmonization. Provide two different chorale-style realizations for each of the following melodies.

Berkov/Stepanov

Exercise 21.10 continued

UNIT 22　Stylized Harmony

Richard Wagner[22]

Parsifal

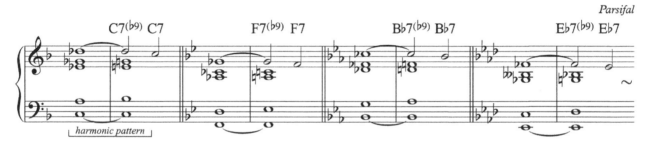

Exercise 22.1.1 Common-tone elaboration of the dominant 7th. Continue up a minor 2nd.

Sigfried

Exercise 22.1.2 Inverted dominant 7th and appoggiatura chords. Continue through all keys.

Exercise 22.1.3 Elaboration of the dominant 9th. Continue through all keys.

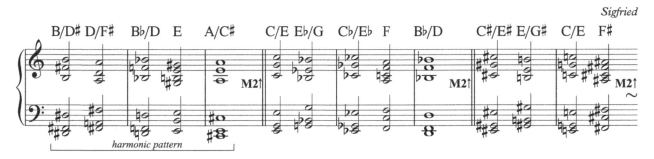

Exercise 22.1.4 *Wotan* chords. Continue through all keys.

Exercise 22.1.5 Semitonal voice leading with the augmented triad. Continue up a minor 2nd.

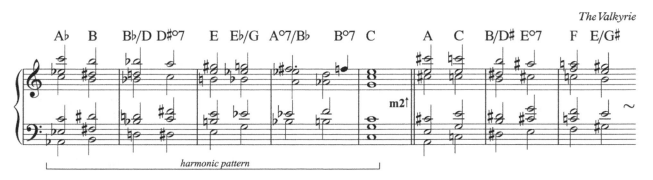

Exercise 22.1.6 *Sleeping* chords. Continue through all keys.

Tristan and Isolda

harmonic pattern

Exercise 22.1.7 Semitonal approach to the dominant. Continue through all keys.

The Meistersingers of Nürnberg

harmonic pattern

Exercise 22.1.8 Inverted dominant 7th and appoggiatura chords. Continue through all keys.

Tristan and Isolda

harmonic pattern

Exercise 22.1.9 Pedal point and a semitonal approach to the tonic. Analyze and continue through all keys.

Tristan and Isolda

harmonic pattern

Exercise 22.1.10 Chromatic sequence. Analyze and continue the sequence up a major 2nd.

Gabriel Fauré

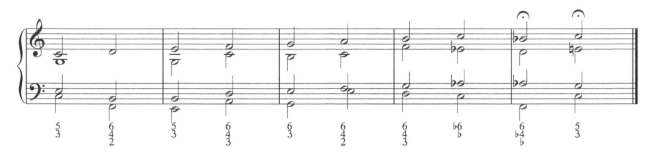

Exercise 22.2.1 **Diatonic *règle à la* Fauré.** Transpose to three keys.

Exercise 22.2.2 **Chromatic *règle à la* Fauré.** Transpose to three keys.

Exercise 22.2.3 **Chromatic dominant expansion.** Transpose to three keys.

Exercise 22.2.4 **Extended V—I cadence.** Analyze and transpose to three keys.

Exercise 22.2.5 **Chromatic approach to the tonic.** Analyze and transpose to three keys.

Exercise 22.2.6 **Chromatic expansion of the lowered submediant.** Analyze and transpose to three keys.

Exercise 22.2.7 **Fauré's progression.** Analyze and continue through all keys.

C   G♭7/D♭ G¹³   C   F   C♭7/G♭ C¹³   F   B♭   F♭7/C♭ F¹³   B♭

Exercise 22.2.8 **Fauré's *Chopin* chord.** Continue through all keys.

D♭7/A♭ B♭m/A♭ G7   E♭9   C♭7/G♭ A♭m/G♭ F7   D♭9   A♭m/G♭   F♯°7   G   C

G♭7/D♭ E♭m/D♭ C7   A♭9   F♭7/C♭ D♭m/C♭ B♭7   G♭9   D♭m/C♭   B°7   C   F

Exercise 22.2.9 Tritone and third related harmonies. Continue through all keys.

D/C   A♭7   G/F   D♭7 B♭m/D♭   E/D   B♭7   A/G   E♭7 Cm/E♭

Exercise 22.2.10 Chromatic sequence. Continue through all keys.

Claude Debussy[23]

Pélleas and Mélisande

Exercise 22.3.1 Chromatic parallel harmony. Analyze and continue through all keys.

le Balcon

F7/G F♯7/G   G9   G7   B♭7/C B7/C   C9   C7   E♭7/F E7/F   F9   F7

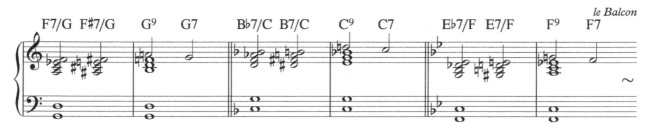

Exercise 22.3.2 Chromatic expansion of dominant 7th. Continue through all keys.

Pélleas and Mélisande

Exercise 22.3.3 Chromatic sequential progression. Transpose to three keys.

Pélleas and Mélisande

Exercise 22.3.4 Augmented triads in harmonic progressions. Transpose to three keys.

Pélleas and Mélisande

Exercise 22.3.5 *Golaud* cadence. Continue through all keys.

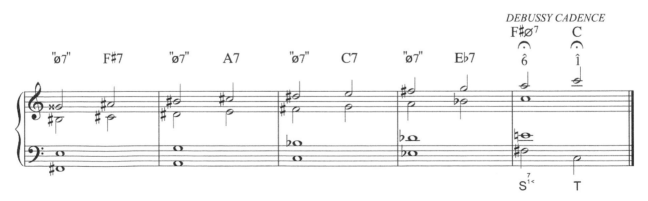

Exercise 22.3.6 Appoggiatura chords and *Debussy* cadence. Transpose to three keys.

Pélleas and Mélisande

Exercise 22.3.7 Tonic pedal point and *Debussy* cadence. Analyze and transpose to three keys.

Prelude to an afternoon of a Faun

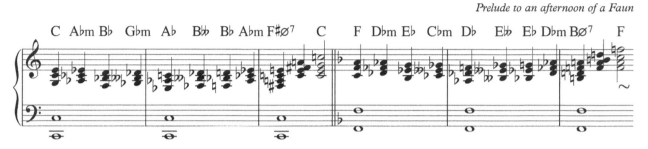

C Abm Bb Gbm Ab Bb Bb Abm F#ø7   C   F Dbm Eb Cbm Db   Eb Eb Dbm Bø7   F

Exercise 22.3.8 Chromatic upper-structure triads. Continue through all keys.

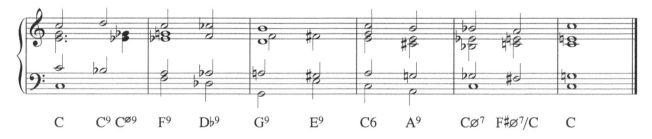

C   C9 Cø9   F9   Db9   G9   E9   C6   A9   Cø7 F#ø7/C   C

Exercise 22.3.9 Chromatic progression with dominant 9th chords. Transpose to three keys.

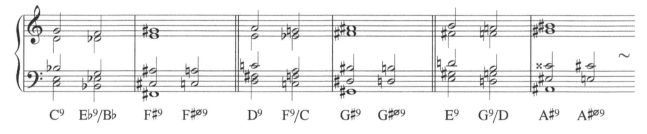

C9   Eb9/Bb   F#9   F#ø9   D9   F9/C   G#9   G#ø9   E9   G9/D   A#9   A#ø9

Exercise 22.3.10 Chromatic sequence. Continue through all keys.

Alexander Scriabin

Exercise 22.4.1 **Inverted altered dominant 7th.** Continue through all keys.

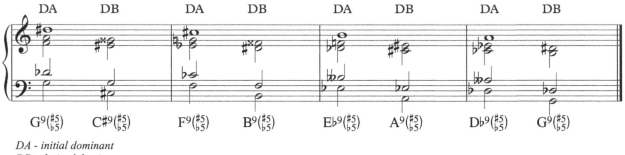

DA - initial dominant
DB - derived dominant

Exercise 22.4.2 **Tritone nucleus: major enharmonic sequence.**[24] Transpose up a minor 2nd.

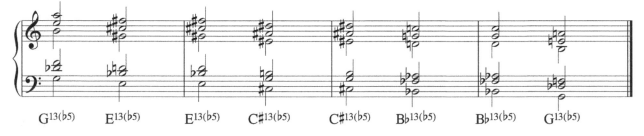

Exercise 22.4.3 **Minor enharmonic sequence.** Transpose down a minor 2nd.

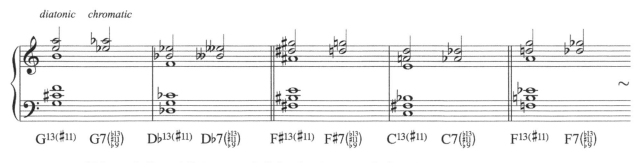

Exercise 22.4.4 **"Diatonic" and "chromatic" Scriabin chord.** Continue through all keys.

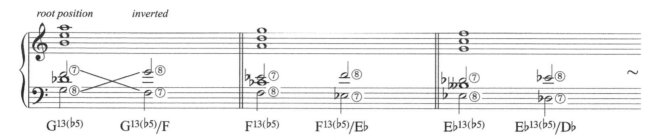

root position   inverted

G¹³(♭5)   G¹³(♭5)/F   F¹³(♭5)   F¹³(♭5)/E♭   E♭¹³(♭5)   E♭¹³(♭5)/D♭

Exercise 22.4.5 **"Inversion" of the *Promethean* chord.** Continue through all keys.

Max Reger[25]

Op. 82 No. 4

Exercise 22.5.1 **Chromatic sequence.** Analyze and continue through all keys.

Op. 60

Exercise 22.5.2 **Reger's Neapolitan.** Continue through all keys.

Op. 80 No. 3

Exercise 22.5.3 **Chromatic tonic expansion.** Analyze and continue through all keys.

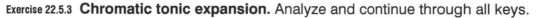

Op. 69 No. 3

Exercise 22.5.4 Tonic pedal point. Analyze and continue through all keys.

Op. 129 No. 7

Exercise 22.5.5 Chromatic progression. Analyze and transpose to three keys.

Op. 60

Exercise 22.5.6 Chromatic progression. Analyze and transpose to three keys.

Op. 60

Exercise 22.5.7 **Chromatic progression.** Analyze and transpose to three keys.

Op. 113

Exercise 22.5.8 **Enharmonic progression.** Analyze and transpose to three keys.

Op. 129 No. 6

Exercise 22.5.9 **Chromatic progression.** Analyze and transpose to three keys.

Op. 127

Exercise 22.5.10 Chromatic progression. Analyze and transpose to three keys.

Olivier Messiaen[26]

Exercise 22.6.1 Harmonic pattern—Mode 2¹. Transpose to Modes 2² and 2³.

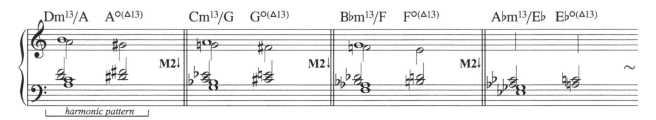

Exercise 22.6.2 Harmonic pattern—Mode 2³. Transpose to Modes 2¹ and 2².

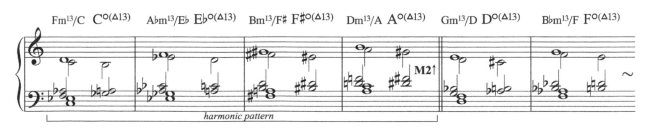

Exercise 22.6.3 Harmonic pattern—Mode 2³. Transpose to Modes 2¹ and 2².

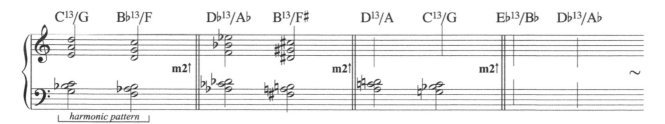

Exercise 22.6.4 **Harmonic pattern with inverted dominant 13ths.** Continue through all keys.

Exercise 22.6.5 **Cyclic harmonic patterns (3-cycle).** Start the pattern on C and B.

Exercise 22.6.6 **The chord on the dominant (*accord sur dominante*).** Continue through all keys.

Exercise 22.6.7 **The chord on the dominant with appoggiatura (*accord sur dominante appoggiaturé*).** Continue through all keys.

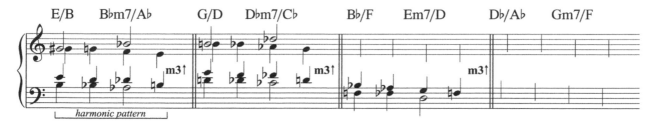

Exercise 22.6.8 **Mode 2².** Transpose to Modes 2¹ and 2³.

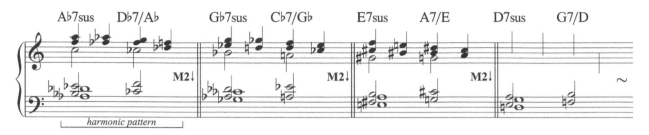

Exercise 22.6.9 Cycle of dominant 7ths. Continue through all keys.

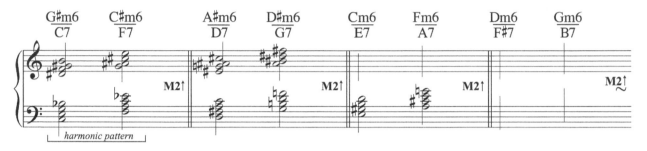

Exercise 22.6.10 The chord of resonance (*accord de la résonance*). Continue through all keys.

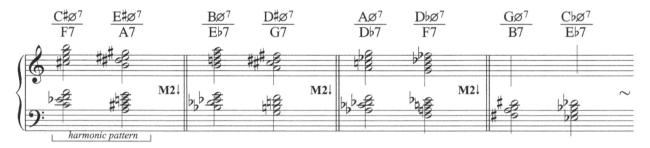

Exercise 22.6.11 The *Arc-en-ciel d'innocence*. Continue the progression and then transpose it up a minor 2nd.

Exercise 22.6.12 A chromatic dominant 7th expansion. Continue through all keys.

Exercise 22.6.13 **A chromatic dominant 7th expansion.** Continue through all keys.

Exercise 22.6.14 **Chords of the transposed inversions (*accord a renversements transposes sur la même de basse*).** Continue through all keys.

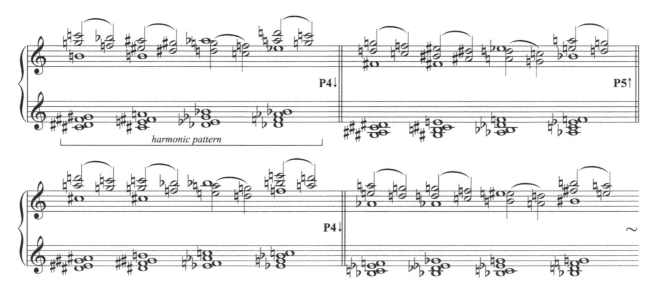

Exercise 22.6.15 **Chords of the transposed inversions with appoggiaturas.** Continue through all keys according to the specific intervallic pattern.

NOTES

1. For a discussion of the lead sheet notation, consult Chapter 3 of *Jazz Theory—From Basic to Advanced Study*.
2. For a discussion of triads, consult Chapter 3 of *Jazz Theory—From Basic to Advanced Study*.
3. In addition to the lead sheet notation, selected exercises will additionally include the functional notation symbols as partially explained in Chapter 3 of *Jazz Theory—From Basic to Advanced Study* and fully discussed in Hugo Riemann's *Harmony Simplified* (*Vereinfachte Harmonielehre*), 1893.
4. See Units 16 and 17 in Appendix B.
5. For a discussion of the Roman numeral notation, consult Chapter 3 of *Jazz Theory—From Basic to Advanced Study*.
6. Since the functional behavior of a major triad in second inversion has been the subject of many a theoretical polemic (some consider it a tonic chord, others a dominant, still others a dissonant chord with one or more suspensions), in this publication we will label that dissonant chord in two different ways depending on the harmonic context in which it occurs: (1) P6/4 and (2) Cad6/4. The former label indicates its passing function and the latter indicates its cadential function.
7. For a discussion of the figured-bass notation, consult Chapter 3 of *Jazz Theory—From Basic to Advanced Study*.
8. For a highly informative and succinct discussion of the practical application of various techniques of cadential evasion, consult Chapter 54 in Gioseffo Zarlino's *Le istitutioni harmoniche* (1558), translated as *The Art of Counterpoint Part III of Le istitutioni harmoniche* (Norton, 1976).
9. At the end of this progression, there is a characteristic cadential closure, which French professor of harmony Henry Challan labeled as the Fauré cadence. That cadential gesture foreshadows the arrival of the tonic chord using two imperfect sonorities: (1) IV⁶ and (2) V⁶₅, with a melodic ascend in the bass voice: $\hat6$–$\hat7$–$\hat1$.
10. Since the functional status of the Tristan chord is highly ambiguous and controversial, the author decided not to add to the existing plethora of theoretical speculations by Karl Meyrberger, Simon Sechter, Hugo Riemann, Sigfried Karg-Elert, Ernst Kurth, Salomon Jadassohn, Cyrill Kistler, Hermann Erpf, Georg Capellen, Alfred Lorenz, Kazimierz Sikorski, John Rahn, and many others regarding its harmonic function.
11. For the discussion of *la règle de l'octave*, consult Chapter 21 of *Jazz Theory—From Basic to Advanced Study*.
12. In this realization, the author demonstrates the use of *class one* consonant voicing formations.
13. At the beginning of the 17th century, the Rule of the Octave occurred in the hexachordal form, demonstrating the centuries-old dominance of the hexachordal pitch space in modal theory and composition. Diruta uses the natural hexachord as a subject for exploring the concepts of melodic diminution, invertible counterpoint, and improvisation.
14. Similar to Diruta's use of the natural hexachord, Spiridionis implements the incomplete Rule of the Octave for the purpose of teaching improvisation. What he calls *Cadentia Secunda* is followed by the 62 (!) creative elaborations of the natural hexachord. See Spiridionis a Monte Carmelo (1615–1685), *Nova Instructio* (ed. Edoardo Bellotti, Il Levante Libreria Editrice, 2018).
15. In this realization of the octave (as in the Fenaroli below), the figured-bass notation indicates the exact positions of the chords in the R.H. The top number indicates the chord member occurring in the soprano voice, the middle number the content of the alto voice, and the bottom number the content of the tenor voice.
16. For a comprehensive discussion of the chaconne and passacaglia, consult Richard Hudson's *The Folia, the Saraband, The Passacaglia, and the Chaconne*, Vol. III and Vol. IV.
17. For an exhaustive and highly informative discussion of galant schematas, see Robert Gjergingen's *Music in the Galant Style* (Oxford, 2007). Many of these harmonic formulas come from his seminal publication.
18. For a comprehensive discussion of partimenti, see Giorgio Sanguinetti's *The Art of Partimento—History, Theory, and Practice* (Oxford, 2012).
19. For an exhaustive study of the omnibus progression, see Victor Fell Yellin's *The Omnibus Idea* (Harmonic Park Press, 1998).
20. In some cases, certain lead-sheet symbols are shown in a simplified form with some pitches enharmonically respelled to facilitate their realization.
21. The following harmonic settings (25 total) come from Théodore Dubois's *Notes & Études d'harmonie pour servir de supplément au traité de H. Reber* (1889). These harmonizations were frequently used by Olivier Messiaen in his harmony lectures.
22. All exercises are derived from Wagner's compositions (where indicated) and occur in a simplified/modified version.
23. All exercises are derived from Debussy's compositions (where indicated) and occur in a simplified/modified version.
24. The terms initial dominant (DA), derived dominant (DB), tritone nucleus, etc. were developed by the Russian theorist Barbara Dernova who, under the tutelage of Boleslav Jaworsky, made significant contributions to the understanding of Scriabin's harmony.
25. All exercises are derived from Reger's compositions (where indicated) and occur in a simplified/modified version.
26. In keeping with Olivier Messiaen's nomenclature used in his theoretical writings, the Modes of Limited Transposition will be labeled using two sets of Arabic numbers: (1) regular size numbers from 1 to 7 indicating seven modes and (2) Arabic numbers in superscript indicating the exact transposition of a mode. For instance, Mode 1 (whole-tone scale) comes in two distinct transpositions, which will be labeled as Mode 1¹ and Mode 1². Mode 2 (with the recurring intervallic pattern of minor and major 2nds: 1/2) comes in three transpositions, which will be labeled as Mode 2¹ (on C), Mode 2² (on C♯), and Mode 2³ (on D).

Appendix C
Jazz Harmony at the Keyboard

MASTER THE FUNDAMENTALS

UNIT 1   Four-Part Chords[1]

MAJOR CHORDS

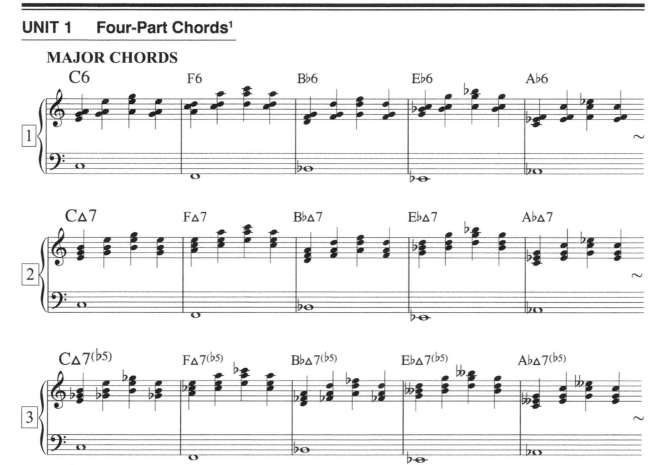

Exercise 1.1 **Four-part chords in all positions.** Continue through all keys.

MINOR CHORDS

DOMINANT CHORDS

Exercise 1.1 continued

HALF-DIMINISHED/DIMINISHED CHORDS

Exercise 1.1 continued

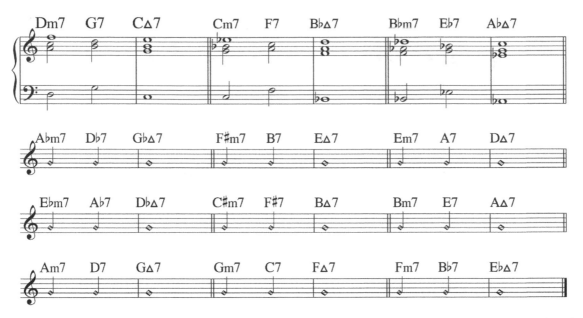

Exercise 1.2 The ii—V⁷—I progression with diatonic chords. Play 3x beginning with (1) a 3rd in the soprano, (2) a 5th in the soprano, and (3) a 7th in the soprano. Continue through all keys.

Exercise 1.3 The ii—V⁷—I progression with chromatic chords. Invert the content of the right hand (R.H.). Continue through all keys.

Exercise 1.4 Harmonic sequences: four-part chords in root position. Play 3x beginning with (1) a 3rd in the soprano, (2) a 5th in the soprano, and (3) a 7th in the soprano. Transpose up a minor second.

Fm7 Bbm7 Ebm7 Abm7 C#m7 F#m7 Bm7 Em7 Am7 Dm7 Gm7 Cm7

F7 Bb7 Eb7 Ab7 Db7 Gb7 B7 E7 A7 D7 G7 C7

F7(#5) Bb7(b5) Eb7(#5) Ab7(b5) Db7(#5) Gb7(b5) B7(#5) E7(b5) A7(#5) D7(b5) G7(#5) C7(b5)

Exercise 1.4 continued

Am7 D7/A Gm7 C7/G Fm7 Bb7/F D#m7 G#7/D# C#m7 F#7/C# Bm7 E7/B

AΔ7 DΔ7/F# GΔ7 CΔ7/E FΔ7 BbΔ7/D EbΔ7 AbΔ7/C C#Δ7 F#Δ7/A# BΔ7 EΔ7/G#

FΔ7/C Bb7sus EbΔ7/Bb Ab7sus DbΔ7/Ab Gb7sus BΔ7/F# E7sus AΔ7/E D7sus GΔ7/D C7sus

Exercise 1.5 Harmonic sequences: four-part chords in inversions. Perform according to the following guidelines: (1) as written; (2) invert the content of the R.H.; (3) invert the content of the L.H.; and (4) invert the content of both hands.[2] Transpose up a minor second.

UNIT 2   Five-Part Chords[3]

MAJOR CHORDS

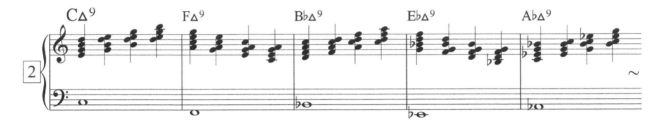

Exercise 2.1 **Five-part chords in all positions.** Continue through all keys.

MINOR CHORDS

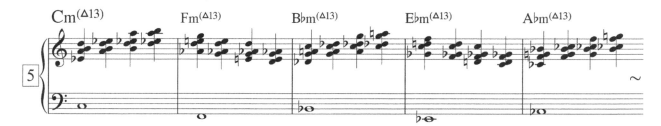

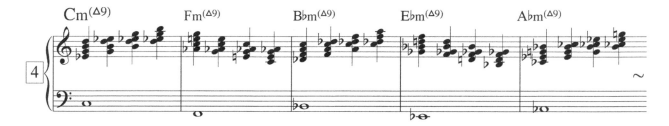

HALF-DIMINISHED/DIMINISHED CHORDS

Exercise 2.1 continued

Exercise 2.1 continued

DOMINANTS WITH MAJOR 9TH (9)

Exercise 2.2 Five-part dominant 7ths in all positions. Continue through all keys.

DOMINANTS WITH MINOR 9TH (♭9)

DOMINANTS WITH AUGMENTED 9TH (♯9)

Exercise 2.2 continued

Exercise 2.2 continued

SUSPENDED DOMINANTS WITH MAJOR 9TH (9)

Exercise 2.3 **Five-part suspended dominant 7ths in all positions.** Continue through all keys.

SUSPENDED DOMINANTS WITH MINOR 9TH (♭9)

Exercise 2.3 continued

SUSPENDED DOMINANTS WITH AUGMENTED 9TH (#9)

Exercise 2.3 continued

MAJOR CHORDS

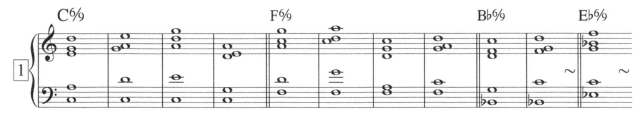

Exercise 2.4 **"Drop 2" voicings in all positions.** Continue through all keys.

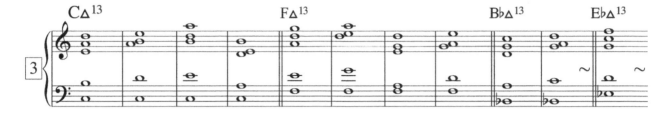

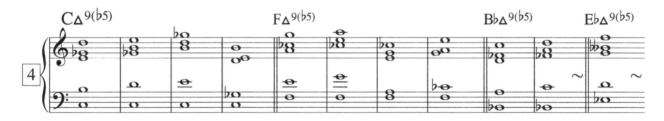

MINOR CHORDS

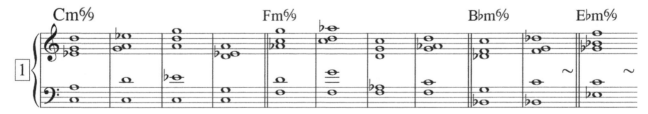

Exercise 2.4 continued

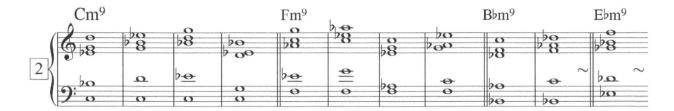

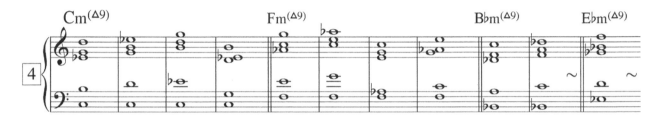

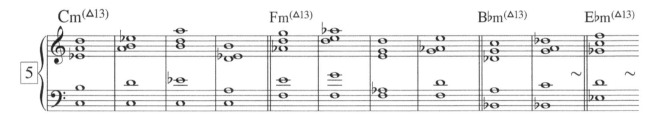

HALF-DIMINISHED/DIMINISHED CHORDS

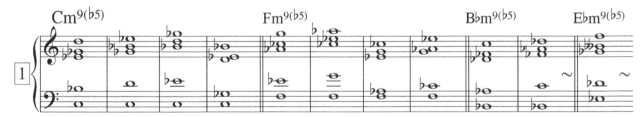

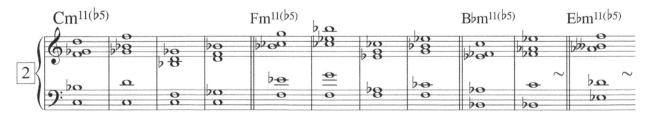

Exercise 2.4 continued

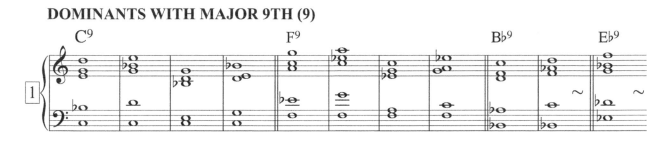

Exercise 2.4 continued

DOMINANTS WITH MAJOR 9TH (9)

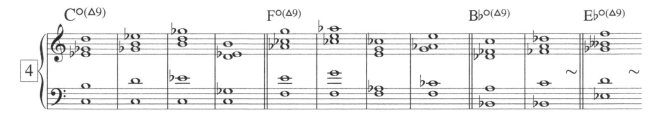

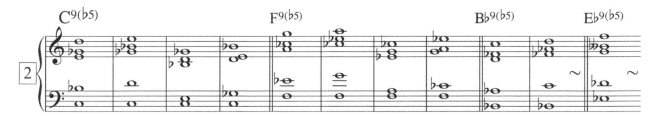

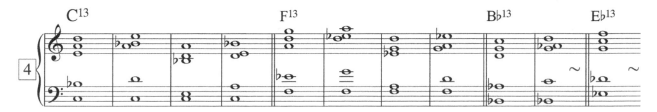

Exercise 2.5 **"Drop 2" dominant 7th voicings in all positions.** Continue through all keys.

DOMINANTS WITH MINOR 9TH (♭9)

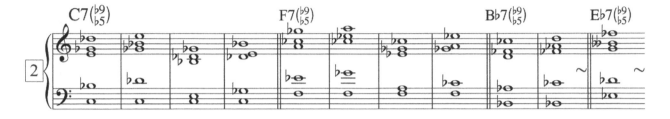

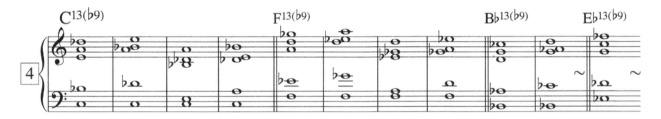

DOMINANTS WITH AUGMENTED 9TH (♯9)

Exercise 2.5 continued

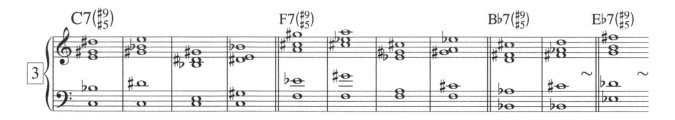

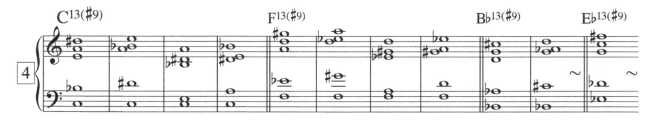

Exercise 2.5 continued

SUSPENDED DOMINANTS WITH MAJOR 9TH (9)

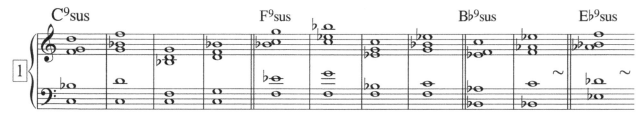

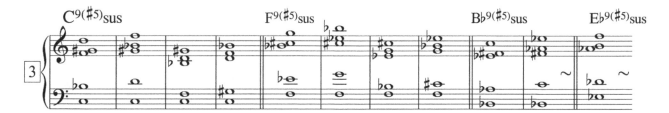

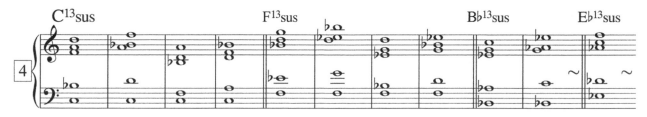

Exercise 2.6 "Drop 2" suspended dominant 7th voicings in all positions. Continue through all keys.

SUSPENDED DOMINANTS WITH MINOR 9TH (♭9)

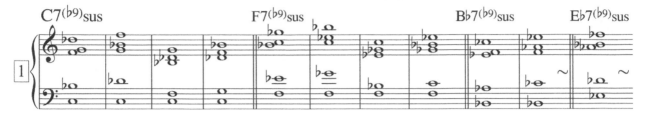

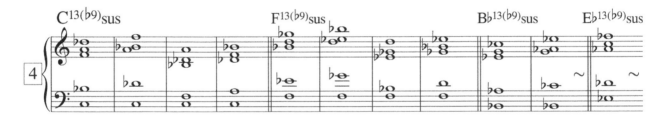

SUSPENDED DOMINANTS WITH AUGMENTED 9TH (♯9)

Exercise 2.6 continued

Exercise 2.6 continued

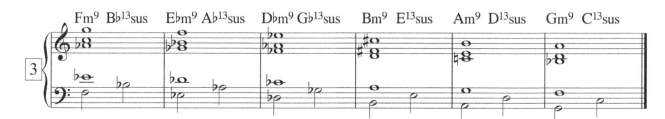

Exercise 2.7 Harmonic sequences: five-part chords in root position. Perform as written and in two remaining positions in the R.H.[4] Transpose up a minor second.

UNIT 3   Six-Part Chords[5]

MAJOR SIX-PART CHORDS

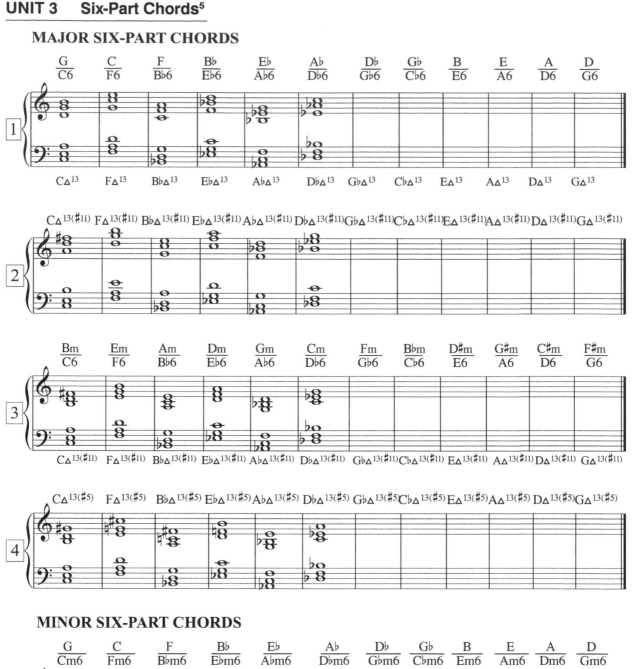

MINOR SIX-PART CHORDS

Exercise 3.1 **Six-part chords with upper-structure triads.** Transpose all chords through the cycle of fifths.

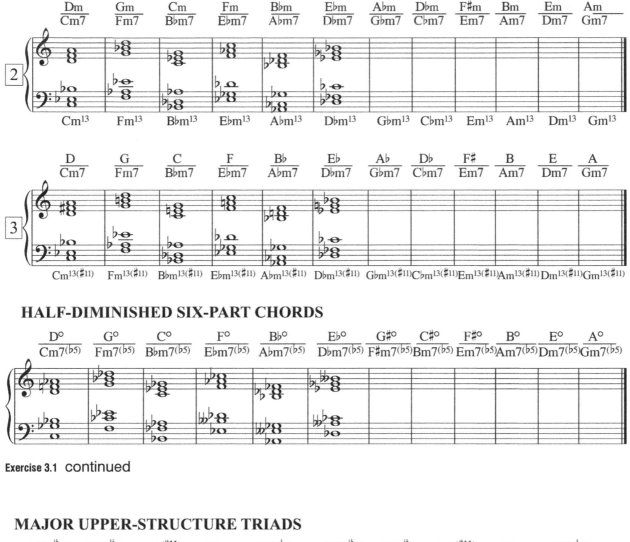

HALF-DIMINISHED SIX-PART CHORDS

Exercise 3.1 continued

MAJOR UPPER-STRUCTURE TRIADS

Exercise 3.2 Six-part dominant 7ths with upper-structure triads. Perform as written and in two remaining inversions in the R.H.[6] Continue through all keys.

MINOR UPPER-STRUCTURE TRIADS

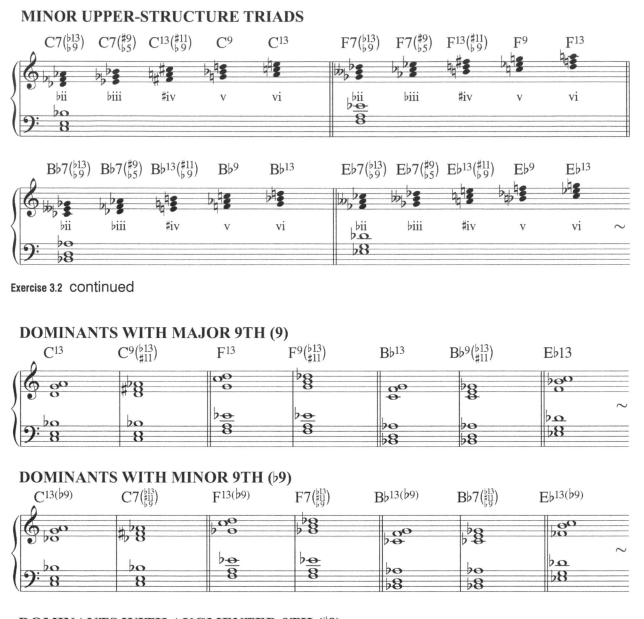

Exercise 3.2 continued

DOMINANTS WITH MAJOR 9TH (9)

DOMINANTS WITH MINOR 9TH (♭9)

DOMINANTS WITH AUGMENTED 9TH (♯9)

DOMINANTS WITH MINOR 9TH (♭9) AND AUGMENTED 9TH (♯9)

Exercise 3.3 Six-part dominant 7ths. Continue through all keys.

MAJOR UPPER-STRUCTURE TRIADS

Exercise 3.4 Resolutions of upper-structure triads in major. Transpose to all keys.

MINOR UPPER-STRUCTURE TRIADS

Exercise 3.4 continued

MAJOR UPPER-STRUCTURE TRIADS

Exercise 3.5 Resolutions of upper-structure triads in minor. Transpose to all keys.

MINOR UPPER-STRUCTURE TRIADS

Exercise 3.5 continued

Exercise 3.6 **The V⁷—I progression with suspended dominant 7ths.** Perform as written and in two remaining positions in the R.H.⁷ Continue through all keys.

Exercise 3.6 continued

Exercise 3.7 The V⁷—I progression with seven-part chords. Perform as written and in two remaining positions in the R.H.[8] Continue through all keys.

Exercise 3.7 continued

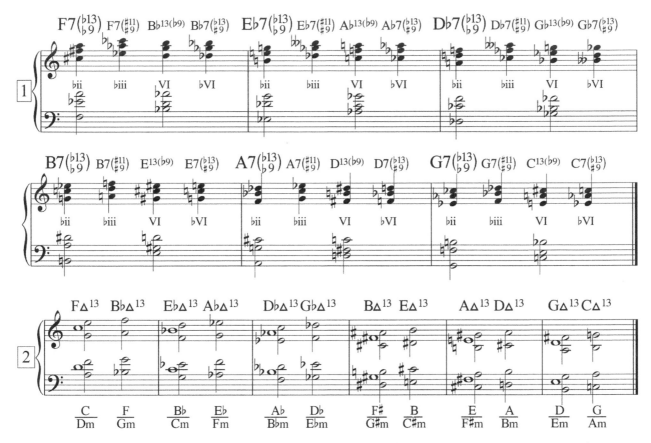

Exercise 3.8 Harmonic sequences: upper-structure triads. Transpose up a minor second.

Exercise 3.9 Harmonic sequences: six-part chords. Transpose up a minor second.

UNIT 4 Jazz Rule of the Octave[9]

Exercise 4.1 **Major scale.** Continue through the cycle of fifths.

C6 D°7 C6/E F°7 C6/G A♭°7 C6/A B°7 C6   C6 B°7 C6/A A♭°7 C6/G F°7 C6/E D°7 C6

F6 G°7 F6/A B♭°7 F6/C D♭°7 F6/D E°7 F6   F6 E°7 F6/D D♭°7 F6/C B♭°7 F6/A G°7 F6

C6 D°7 C6/E F°7 C6/G A♭°7 C6/A B°7 C6   C6 B°7 C6/A A♭°7 C6/G F°7 C6/E D°7 C6

F6 G°7 F6/A B♭°7 F6/C D♭°7 F6/D E°7 F6   F6 E°7 F6/D D♭°7 F6/C B♭°7 F6/A G°7 F6

Exercise 4.2 Major bebop scale. Continue through the cycle of fifths.

MAJOR PENTATONIC

C6/9

F6/9

B♭6/9

E♭6/9

Exercise 4.3 Pentatonic scales. Continue through the cycle of fifths.

MINOR PENTATONIC

DOMINANT PENTATONIC

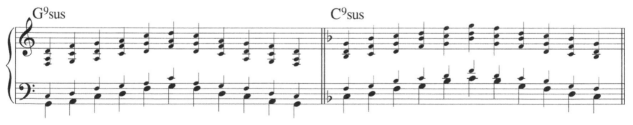

SUSPENDED PENTATONIC

Exercise 4.3 continued

MAJOR SCALE

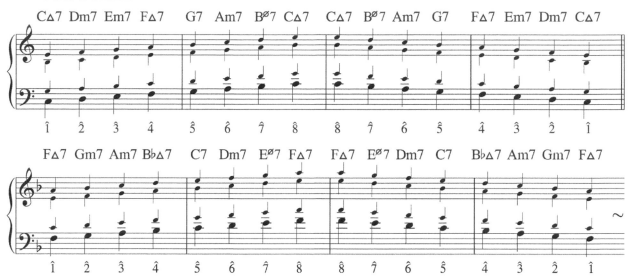

Exercise 4.4 Four-part chorale texture. Perform according to the following guidelines: (1) as written; (2) invert the content of the R.H.; (3) invert the content of the L.H.; and (4) invert the content of both hands.[10] Continue through the cycle of fifths.

DORIAN MODE

Exercise 4.5 Dorian voicings. Continue through all Dorian modes.

AEOLIAN MODE

Exercise 4.6 Aeolian voicings. Continue through all Aeolian modes.

PHRYGIAN MODE

Exercise 4.7 Phrygian voicings. Continue through all Phrygian modes.

LOCRIAN MODE

Exercise 4.8 Locrian voicings. Continue through all Locrian modes.

IONIAN MODE

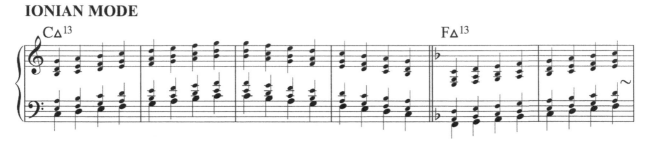

Exercise 4.9 Ionian voicings. Continue through all Ionian modes.

MIXOLYDIAN MODE

Exercise 4.10 Mixolydian voicings *a là* Messiaen (*accord sur dominante*). Continue through all Mixolydian modes.

LYDIAN MODE

Exercise 4.11 Lydian voicings. Continue through all Lydian modes.

MODE 2[1]

Exercise 4.12 Octatonic scale 2[1] (1/2).[11] Continue through all octatonic scales.

UNIT 5   The II—V—I Progression[12]

Exercise 5.1 The ii—V[7]—I progression with five-part chords. Play 4x beginning with (1) a 3rd in the soprano; (2) a 5th in the soprano; (3) a 7th in the soprano; and (4) a 9th in the soprano. Continue through all keys.

Exercise 5.2 The iiø—V⁷—i progression with five-part chords. Play 4x beginning with (1) a diminished 5th in the soprano; (2) a 7th in the soprano; (3) a 9th in the soprano; and (4) a 3rd in the soprano. Continue through all keys.

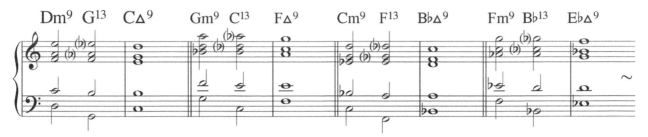

Exercise 5.3 Five-part chorale texture. Play 3x beginning with (1) a 9th in the soprano; (2) a 3rd in the soprano; and (3) a 5th in the soprano. Modify dominant chords using (1) ♭9; (2) ♭13; or (3) ♭9/♭13. Continue through all keys.

Exercise 5.4 The ii—V⁷—I progression with five-part chords. Continue as written and in the remaining three "drop 2" positions. Continue through all keys.

Exercise 5.5 Three-part texture. Continue through all keys.

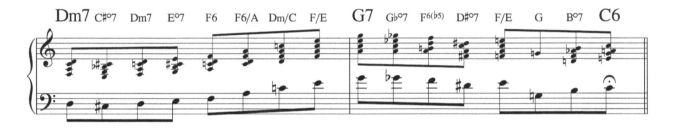

Exercise 5.6 Locked-hand style. Continue through all keys.

FUNDAMENTALS TO MASTERY

UNIT 6   Idiomatic Jazz Progressions[13]

1	Dm7	G7	CΔ7	C6
2	Dm7	G7 D♭7	CΔ7	C6
3	D7	G7	CΔ7	C6
4	A♭7	G7	CΔ7	C6
5	A♭7	D♭7	CΔ7	C6

Exercise 6.1 Harmonic transformations of ii—V⁷—I. Realize the following progressions in keyboard texture (Model I, II, III, IV, V, and VI) and chorale texture: (1) five-part: 3 + 2, (2) "drop 2," and (3) four-part with incomplete chords. Transpose to all keys.[14]

6	A♭7	A♭m7　D♭7	CΔ7	C6
7	E♭m7　A♭7	Dm7　G7	CΔ7	C6
8	D7　A♭7	G7	CΔ7	C6
9	D7　A♭7	G7　D♭7	CΔ7	C6
10	E♭m7　A♭7	A♭m7　D♭7	CΔ7	C6
11	Dm7　E♭m7　A♭7	G7　A♭m7　D♭7	CΔ7	C6
12	Dm7　A♭7	E♭m7　A♭7　Dm7　D♭7	CΔ7	C6
13	D7　E♭m7　A♭7	A♭m7　D♭7　D7　D♭7	CΔ7	C6
14	D7　E♭m7　A♭7	D7　A♭7　G7　D♭7	CΔ7	C6

Exercise 6.1 continued

Modulations to closely related keys

1	I	ii—V⁷	(ii—V⁷)/IV	IV
2	I	ii—V⁷	(ii—V⁷)/V	V
3	I	ii—V⁷	(ii—V⁷)/II	II
4	I	ii—V⁷	(ii—V⁷)/♭VII	♭VII
5	I	ii—V⁷	(ii—V⁷)/VI	VI
6	I	ii—V⁷	(ii—V⁷)/♭III	♭III

Modulations to remotely related keys

1	I	ii—V⁷	(ii—V⁷)/III	III
2	I	ii—V⁷	(ii—V⁷)/♭VI	♭VI
3	I	ii—V⁷	(ii—V⁷)/VII	VII
4	I	ii—V⁷	(ii—V⁷)/♭II	♭II
5	I	ii—V⁷	(ii—V⁷)/♯IV	♯IV

Exercise 6.2 Modulatory schemas I. Perform as specified in Exercise 6.1.

Modulations from major to minor

1	I	ii—V⁷	(ii⌀—V⁷)/ii	ii
2	I	ii—V⁷	(ii⌀—V⁷)/vi	vi
3	I	ii—V⁷	(ii⌀—V⁷)/iii	iii
4	I	ii—V⁷	(ii⌀—V⁷)/iv	iv

Exercise 6.3 Modulatory schemas II. Perform as specified in Exercise 6.1.

Modulations from minor to major

1	i	ii$^\varnothing$—V^7	(ii^7—V^7)/**III**	**III**
2	i	ii$^\varnothing$—V^7	(ii^7—V^7)/**VI**	**VI**
3	i	ii$^\varnothing$—V^7	(ii^7—V^7)/**VII**	**VII**
4	i	ii$^\varnothing$—V^7	(ii^7—V^7)/**V**	**V**
5	i	ii$^\varnothing$—V^7	(ii^7—V^7)/♭**II**	♭**II**

Modulations from minor to minor

1	i	ii$^\varnothing$—V^7	(ii$^\varnothing$—V^7)/**iv**	**iv**
2	i	ii$^\varnothing$—V^7	(ii$^\varnothing$—V^7)/**v**	**v**
3	i	ii$^\varnothing$—V^7	(ii$^\varnothing$—V^7)/**ii**	**ii**
4	i	ii$^\varnothing$—V^7	(ii$^\varnothing$—V^7)/**vii**	**vii**
5	i	ii$^\varnothing$—V^7	(ii$^\varnothing$—V^7)/**iii**	**iii**

Exercise 6.3 continued

Modulations with two [ii—V^7]/X interpolations

1	ii—V^7	[ii—V^7]/**IV**	(ii—V^7)/**VII**	**VII**
2	ii—V^7	[ii—V^7]/**VII**	(ii—V^7)/♭**VII**	♭**VII**
3	ii—V^7	[ii—V^7]/♭**V**	(ii—V^7)/**VI**	**VI**
4	ii—V^7	[ii—V^7]/**III**	(ii—V^7)/♭**VI**	♭**VI**
5	ii—V^7	[ii—V^7]/♭**VII**	(ii—V^7)/**V**	**V**
6	ii—V^7	[ii—V^7]/♭**III**	(ii—V^7)/♭**V**	♭**V**
7	ii—V^7	[ii—V^7]/**V**	(ii—V^7)/**IV**	**IV**
8	ii—V^7	[ii—V^7]/♯**IV**	(ii—V^7)/**III**	**III**
9	ii—V^7	[ii—V^7]/**IV**	(ii—V^7)/♭**III**	♭**III**
10	ii—V^7	[ii—V^7]/**III**	(ii—V^7)/**II**	**II**
11	ii—V^7	[ii—V^7]/**II**	(ii—V^7)/♭**II**	♭**II**
12	ii—V^7	[ii—V^7]/**III**	(ii—V^7)/**VII**	**VII**
13	ii—V^7	[ii—V^7]/**II**	(ii—V^7)/♭**VII**	♭**VII**
14	ii—V^7	[ii—V^7]/♭**VI**	(ii—V^7)/**VI**	**VI**
15	ii—V^7	[ii—V^7]/**IV**	(ii—V^7)/♭**VI**	♭**VI**

Exercise 6.4 **Modulatory schemas III.** Perform as specified in Exercise 6.1.

1	ii—V⁷	[ii—V⁷]/**IV**	(ii—V⁷)/**VII**	**VII**
16	ii—V⁷	[ii—V⁷]/♭**III**	(ii—V⁷)/**V**	**V**
17	ii—V⁷	[ii—V⁷]/**VI**	(ii—V⁷)/♭**V**	♭**V**
18	ii—V⁷	[ii—V⁷]/**VI**	(ii—V⁷)/**IV**	**IV**
19	ii—V⁷	[ii—V⁷]/♭**VII**	(ii—V⁷)/**III**	**III**
20	ii—V⁷	[ii—V⁷]/**VII**	(ii—V⁷)/♭**III**	♭**III**
21	ii—V⁷	[ii—V⁷]/#**IV**	(ii—V⁷)/**II**	**II**
22	ii—V⁷	[ii—V⁷]/**V**	(ii—V⁷)/♭**II**	♭**II**

Exercise 6.4 continued

Beginning on I

1	I—vi	ii—V⁷	iii—vi	ii—V⁷
2	I—#i°	ii—#ii°	ii—♭VI⁷	(ii—V⁷)/IV
3	I	(ii—V⁷)/IV	IV	ii—V⁷
4	I	[iiø—V⁷]/vi	(ii—V⁷)/IV	IV
5	I—IV	iii—♭VII⁷	vi—II⁷	ii—Tr/V
6	I	IV—#iv°	I—VI⁷	II⁷—V⁷
7	I—♭V⁷	IV⁷—♭VII⁷	I—VI⁷	II⁷—Tr/V
8	I	#iv°—iv	iii—VI⁷	ii—♭VII⁷
9	I	[iiø—V⁷]/iii	[ii—V⁷]/♭III	ii—V⁷
10	I	(iiø—V⁷)/ii	ii	(iiø—V⁷)/vi
11	I	[ii—V⁷]/♭II	ii—V⁷	I
12	I	[ii—V⁷]/♭VII	[ii—V⁷]/♭VI	ii—V⁷
13	I	(ii—V⁷)/♭VI	♭VI	ii—V⁷

Beginning on II—V

1	ii—V⁷	I—vi	[ii—V⁷]/♭III	ii—Tr/V
2	ii—V⁷	vi—II⁷	iii—♭iii°	ii—V⁷
3	ii—V⁷	[ii—V⁷]/♭III	[ii—V⁷]/♭V	(ii—V⁷)/VI
4	ii—V⁷	[ii—V⁷]/II	vi—II⁷	ii—Tr/V
5	iiø—V⁷	I	[ii—V⁷]/III	ii—V⁷
6	iiø—V⁷	I—♭V⁷	IV⁷—♭VII⁷	I
7	(iiø—V⁷)/iv	iv	ii—V⁷	I

Exercise 6.5 **Four-bar progressions.** Perform as specified in Exercise 6.1.

Beginning on IV

1	IV	[ii—V⁷]/♭III	I	ii—Tr/V
2	IV	ii—V⁷	I—vi	(iiᴼ—V⁷)/vi
3	IV	iii—vi	ii—V⁷	Tr/V
4	IV	♯ivᴼ	I	I
5	IV	[iiᴼ—V⁷]/iii	(iiᴼ—V⁷)/ii	ii—Tr/V
6	IV	(iiᴼ—V⁷)/vi	vi—II⁷	ii—V⁷

Beginning on vi

1	vi	ii	V⁷	I
2	vi	II⁷	ii	Tr/V
3	vi	ii—V⁷	I	(iiᴼ—V⁷)/ii
4	vi	[iiᴼ—V⁷]/vi	(iiᴼ—V⁷)/iii	iii
5	vi	[iiᴼ—V⁷]/vi	[ii—V⁷]/IV	ii—V⁷

Exercise 6.5 continued

FIRST POSITION

SECOND POSITION

THIRD POSITION

Exercise 6.6 The "Giant Steps" progression. Transpose to three keys.

FOURTH POSITION

Exercise 6.6 continued

Exercise 6.7 The "Countdown" progression. Transpose to three keys.

Exercise 6.8 The vi—ii—V⁷—I progressions with diminished 7th chords. Continue through all keys.

UNIT 7 Tritone Substitutions

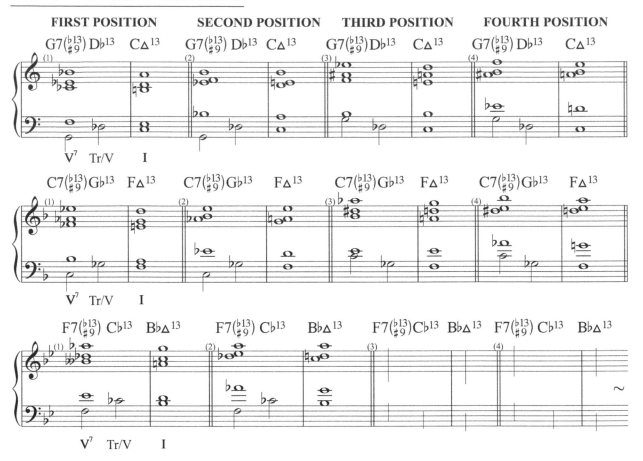

Exercise 7.1 The V⁷—Tr/V—I progression in four positions. Perform as written and in two remaining positions in the R.H.[15] Continue through the cycle of fifths.

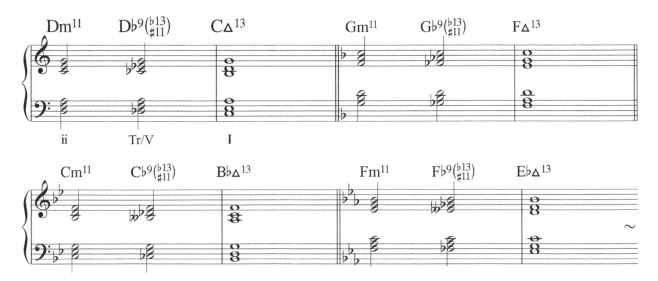

Exercise 7.2 The ii—Tr/V—I progression with six-part chords. Continue through the cycle of fifths.

UNIT 8   Phrase Models[16]

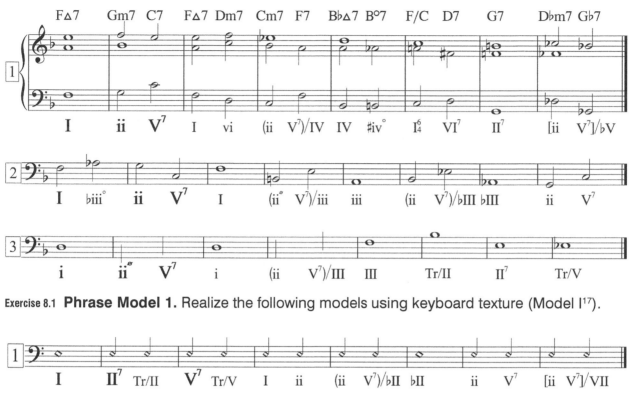

Exercise 8.1 Phrase Model 1. Realize the following models using keyboard texture (Model I[17]).

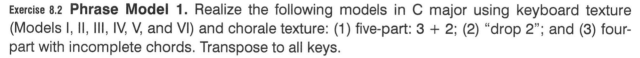

Exercise 8.2 Phrase Model 1. Realize the following models in C major using keyboard texture (Models I, II, III, IV, V, and VI) and chorale texture: (1) five-part: 3 + 2; (2) "drop 2"; and (3) four-part with incomplete chords. Transpose to all keys.

Exercise 8.3 Phrase Model 2. Realize the following models using chorale texture (five-part: 3 + 2 and "drop 2").

1 ii V⁷ I (ii V⁷)/III III [ii V⁷]/♭III iii ♭iii° ii V⁷

2 ii° V⁷ i (ii° V⁷)/iv iv ii° V⁷ i IV⁷ ii° Tr/V i

Exercise 8.4 Phrase Model 2. Realize the following models in G major using keyboard texture (Models I, II, III, IV, V, and VI) and chorale texture: (1) five-part: 3 + 2; (2) "drop 2"; and (3) four-part with incomplete chords. Transpose to all keys.

C△7 Cm7 F7 F♯°7 G△7 Bm7 E7 Am7 B♭°7 Bm7 E7 Am7 D7 Dm7 G7

1 IV [ii V⁷]/♭III vii° I (ii V⁷)/ii ii ♭iii° iii VI⁷ ii V⁷ [ii V⁷]/IV

2 IV [ii V⁷]/VI [ii V⁷]/♭VI [ii V⁷]/V ii Tr/V [ii V⁷]/♭VII [ii V⁷]/♭II ii V⁷

3 IV I IV ♯iv° (ii V⁷)/IV IV I ii V⁷ [ii V⁷]/♭V

Exercise 8.5 Phrase Model 3. Realize the following models using keyboard texture (Model I).

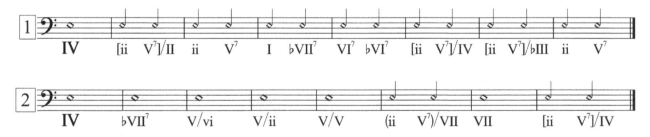

1 IV [ii V⁷]/II ii V⁷ I ♭VII⁷ VI⁷ ♭VI⁷ [ii V⁷]/IV [ii V⁷]/♭III ii V⁷

2 IV ♭VII⁷ V/vi V/ii V/V (ii V⁷)/VII VII [ii V⁷]/IV

Exercise 8.6 Phrase Model 3. Realize the following models in F major using keyboard texture (Models I, II, III, IV, V, and VI) and chorale texture: (1) five-part: 3 + 2; (2) "drop 2"; and (3) four-part with incomplete chords. Transpose to all keys.

Exercise 8.7 Phrase Model 4. Realize the following models using chorale texture (five-part: 3 + 2 and "drop 2").

Exercise 8.8 Phrase Model 4. Realize the following models in D major using keyboard texture (Models I, II, III, IV, V, and VI) and chorale texture: (1) five-part: 3 + 2; (2) "drop 2"; and (3) four-part with incomplete chords. Transpose to all keys.

Exercise 8.9 Phrase Model 5. Realize the following models using keyboard texture (Model IV and VI).

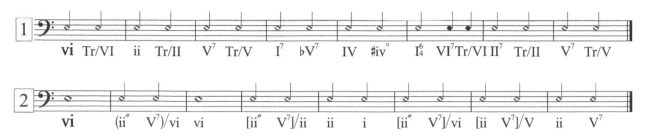

Exercise 8.10 Phrase Model 5. Realize the following models in B♭ major using keyboard texture (Models I, II, III, IV, V, and VI) and chorale texture: (1) five-part: 3 + 2; (2) "drop 2"; and (3) four-part with incomplete chords. Transpose to all keys.

Exercise 8.11 Phrase Model 6. Realize the following models using keyboard texture (Model VI + walking bass).

Exercise 8.12 Phrase Model 6. Realize the following models in A major using keyboard texture (Models I, II, III, IV, V, and VI) and chorale texture: (1) five-part: 3 + 2; (2) "drop 2"; and (3) four-part with incomplete chords. Transpose to all keys.

Exercise 8.13 **Phrase Model 7.** Realize the following models using keyboard texture (Model IV and VI + walking bass).

Exercise 8.14 **Phrase Model 7.** Realize the following models in E♭ major using keyboard texture (Models I, II, III, IV, V, and VI) and chorale texture: (1) five-part: 3 + 2; (2) "drop 2"; and (3) four-part with incomplete chords. Transpose to all keys.

Exercise 8.15 **Phrase Model 8.** Realize the following models using keyboard texture (Model VI).

Exercise 8.16 Phrase Model 8. Realize the following models in E major using keyboard texture (Models I, II, III, IV, V, and VI) and chorale texture: (1) five-part: 3 + 2; (2) "drop 2"; and (3) four-part with incomplete chords. Transpose to all keys.

Exercise 8.17 Phrase Model 9. Realize the following models using chorale texture (five-part: 3 + 2 and "drop 2").

Exercise 8.18 Phrase Model 9. Realize the following models in A♭ major using keyboard texture (Models I, II, III, IV, V, and VI) and chorale texture: (1) five-part: 3 + 2; (2) "drop 2"; and (3) four-part with incomplete chords. Transpose to all keys.

Exercise 8.19 Phrase Model 10. Realize the following models using chorale texture (four-part with incomplete chords).

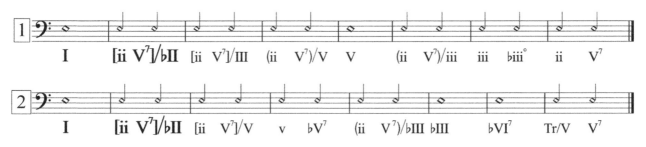

Exercise 8.20 Phrase Model 10. Realize the following models in B major using keyboard texture (Models I, II, III, IV, V, and VI) and chorale texture: (1) five-part: 3 + 2; (2) "drop 2"; and (3) four-part with incomplete chords. Transpose to all keys.

Exercise 8.21 Phrase Model 11. Realize the following models using chorale texture (four-part with incomplete chords).

Exercise 8.22 Phrase Model 11. Realize the following models in D♭ major using keyboard texture (Models I, II, III, IV, V, and VI) and chorale texture: (1) five-part: 3 + 2; (2) "drop 2"; and (3) four-part with incomplete chords. Transpose to all keys.

Exercise 8.23 Phrase Model 12. Realize the following models using chorale texture (four-part with incomplete chords).

Exercise 8.24 Phrase Model 12. Realize the following models in G♭ major using keyboard texture (Models I, II, III, IV, V, and VI) and chorale texture: (1) five-part: 3 + 2; (2) "drop 2"; and (3) four-part with incomplete chords. Transpose to all keys.

Exercise 8.25 Phrase Model 13. Realize the following models using chorale texture (four-part with incomplete chords).

Exercise 8.26 Phrase Model 13. Realize the following models in C major using keyboard texture (Models I, II, III, IV, V, and VI) and chorale texture: (1) five-part: 3 + 2; (2) "drop 2"; and (3) four-part with incomplete chords. Transpose to all keys.

MASTERY TO EXCELLENCE

UNIT 9   Functional Piano Accompaniments

Exercise 9.1 Two-bar turnarounds with walking bass accompaniments. Continue through all keys.

TURNAROUND LADY BIRD

TURNAROUND INNER URGE

TURNAROUND ISOTOPE

Exercise 9.1 continued

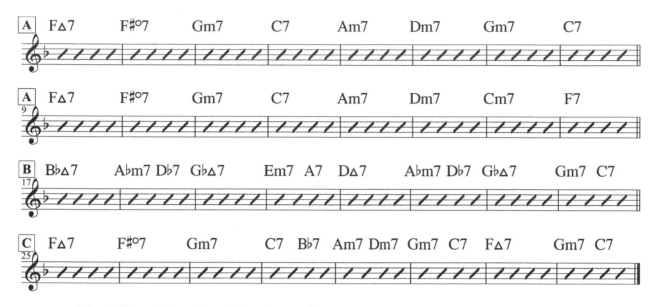

Exercise 9.2 The "Have You Met Miss Jones?" progression. Realize with different models of functional accompaniment from Exercise 9.1.

BOSSA NOVA

PARTIDO ALTO 2:3

BAIÃO

Exercise 9.3 Four-bar turnarounds with straight 8ths accompaniments.[18] Transpose to four additional keys.

CHORINHO

CHA-CHA-CHÁ

BEMBE

BEMBE

MONTUNO 2:3

Exercise 9.3 continued

MONTUNO 3:2

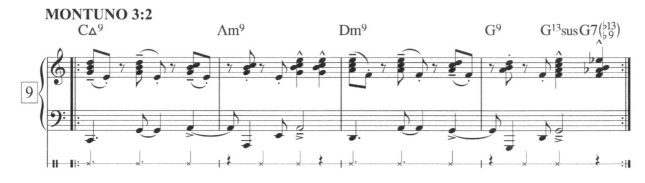

MONTUNO 2:3

MONTUNO 3:2

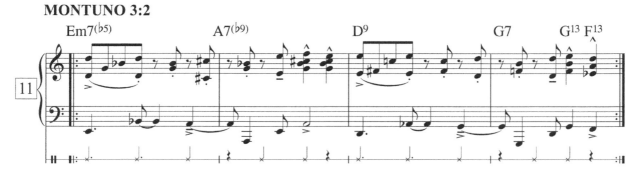

Exercise 9.3 continued

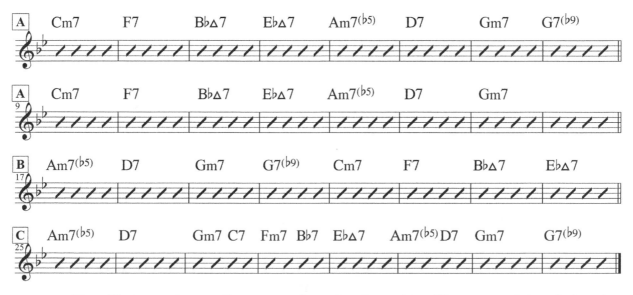

Exercise 9.4 The "Autumn Leaves" progression. Realize with different models of functional accompaniment from Exercise 9.3 using (1) bossa nova; (2) partido alto 2:3; (3) baião; (4) chorinho; (5) cha-cha-chá; (6) bembe 6/8; (7) bembe 12/8; (8) montuno 2:3; and (9) montuno 3:2.

TWO FEEL

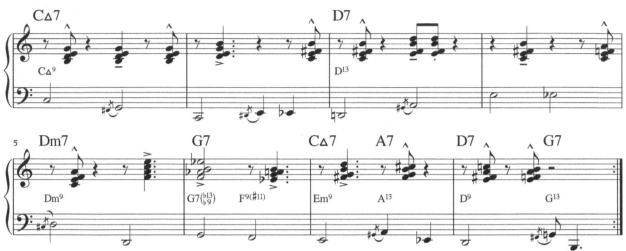

WALKING BASS

STRIDE 1

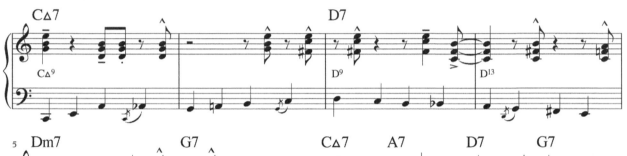

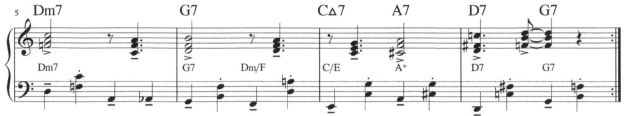

Exercise 9.5 The A section from "Take the A Train" with different accompaniments. Transpose to four additional keys.

STRIDE 2

SAMBA

BOSSA NOVA

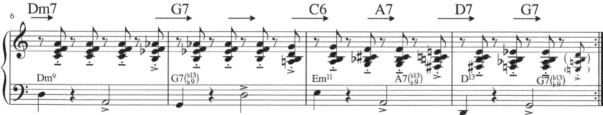

Exercise 9.5 continued

MONTUNO 2:3

Exercise 9.5 continued

Exercise 9.6 The "Green Dolphin Street" progression. Realize with different models of functional accompaniment from Exercise 9.5 using (1) two feel; (2) walking bass; (3) stride 1; (4) stride 2; (5) samba; (6) bossa nova; and (7) montuno 2:3.

UNIT 10 Blues Progressions With Various Accompaniments[19]

Exercise 10.1 **Five-part chorale texture.** Transpose to two additional keys.

Exercise 10.2 **Walking 10ths.** Transpose to two additional keys.

BASIC BLUES

BLUES FOR ALICE

Exercise 10.3 Four-part comping texture with rootless chords. Transpose to two additional keys.

DANCE OF THE INFIDELS

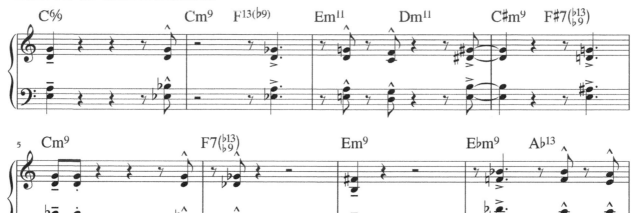

Exercise 10.3 continued

BASIC BLUES

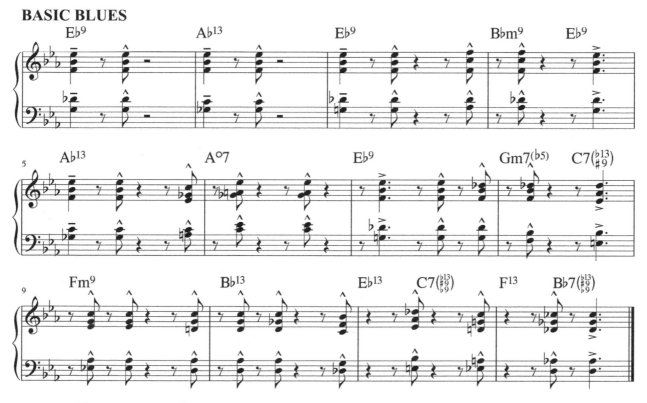

Exercise 10.4 **Five-part comping texture with rootless chords.** Transpose to two additional keys.

BLUES FOR ALICE

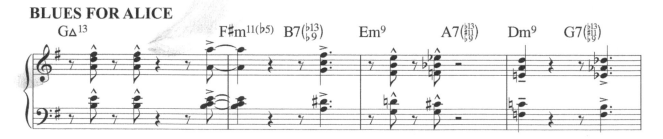

DANCE OF THE INFIDELS

Exercise 10.4 continued

MINOR BLUES

Exercise 10.5 **Modal accompaniment.** Transpose to two additional keys.

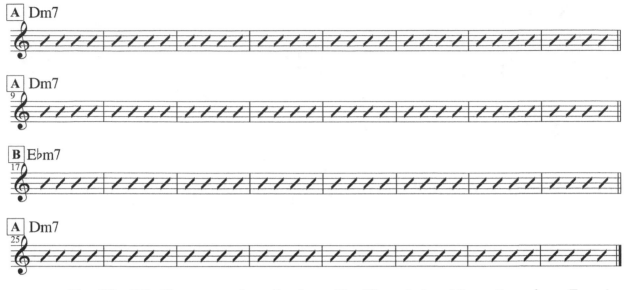

Exercise 10.6 The "So What" progression. Realize with different chord formations from Exercise 10.5.

UNIT 11   The "Confirmation" Changes With Functional Accompaniment[20]

Exercise 11.1 Walking bass. Transpose to two additional keys.

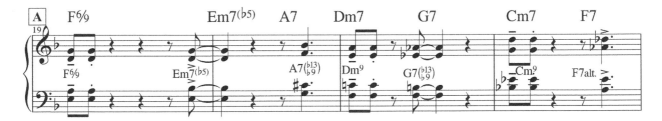

Exercise 11.2 Four-part comping texture with rootless chords. Transpose to two additional keys.

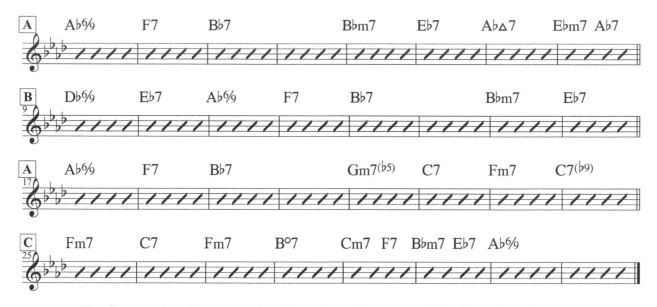

Exercise 11.3 The "Donna Lee" progression. Based on different models of functional accompaniment from Exercises 11.1 and 11.2, realize the following chord progression using (1) walking bass and (2) four-part comping texture.

UNIT 12   The Rhythm Changes Progression With Functional Accompaniment[21]

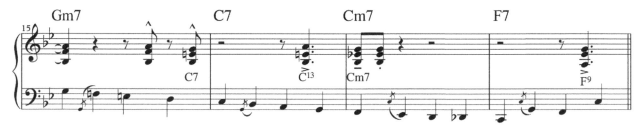

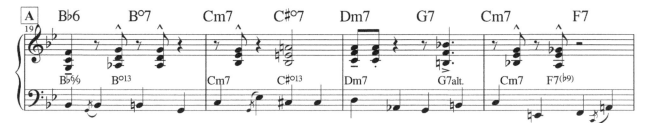

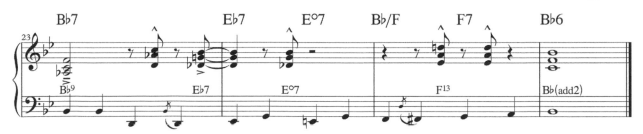

Exercise 12.1 **Walking bass.** Transpose to two additional keys.

Exercise 12.2 Five-part comping texture with rootless chords. Transpose to two additional keys.

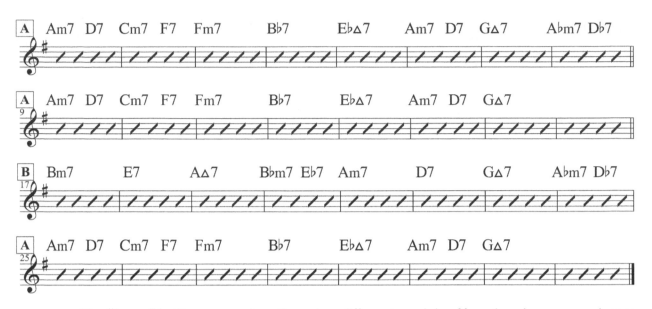

Exercise 12.3 The "Lazy Bird" progression. Based on different models of functional accompaniment from Exercises 12.1 and 12.2, realize the following chord progression using (1) walking bass and (2) five-part comping texture.

NOTES

1. For a discussion of four-part chords, consult Chapter 4 of *Jazz Theory—From Basic to Advanced Study*.
2. Remember that the distance between the lowest note in the R.H. and the highest note in the L.H. cannot exceed an octave.
3. For a discussion of five-part chords, consult Chapter 5 of *Jazz Theory—From Basic to Advanced Study*.
4. Remember that the distance between the lowest note in the R.H. and the highest note in the L.H. cannot exceed an octave.
5. For a discussion of six-part chords, consult Chapter 11 of *Jazz Theory—From Basic to Advanced Study*.
6. Remember that the distance between the lowest note in the R.H. and the highest note in the L.H. cannot exceed an octave.
7. Remember that the distance between the lowest note in the R.H. and the highest note in the L.H. cannot exceed an octave.
8. Remember that the distance between the lowest note in the R.H. and the highest note in the L.H. cannot exceed an octave.
9. For a discussion of the jazz Rule of the Octave, consult Chapter 21 of *Jazz Theory—From Basic to Advanced Study*.
10. Remember that the distance between the lowest note in the R.H. and the highest note in the L.H. cannot exceed an octave.
11. Consult Chapter 23 of *Jazz Theory—From Basic to Advanced Study*.
12. For a discussion of the progression, consult Chapter 6 of *Jazz Theory—From Basic to Advanced Study*.
13. For a discussion of idiomatic progressions, consult Chapter 13 of *Jazz Theory—From Basic to Advanced Study*.
14. For an explanation of keyboard and chorale texture, consult Chapter 12 of *Jazz Theory—From Basic to Advanced Study*.
15. Remember that the distance between the lowest note in the R.H. and the highest note in the L.H. cannot exceed an octave.
16. For a discussion of phrase models, consult Chapter 21 of *Jazz Theory—From Basic to Advanced Study*.
17. For an explanation of keyboard (Models I through VI) and chorale texture, consult Chapter 12 of *Jazz Theory—From Basic to Advanced Study*
18. For a discussion of different rhythms from South America, consult Chapter 2 of *Jazz Theory—From Basic to Advanced Study*.
19. For a discussion of the blues, consult Chapters 9 and 15 of *Jazz Theory—From Basic to Advanced Study*.
20. Consult Chapter 16 of *Jazz Theory—From Basic to Advanced Study*.
21. Consult Chapter 17 of *Jazz Theory—From Basic to Advanced Study*.

Appendix D
Patterns for Jazz Improvisation

MASTER THE FUNDAMENTALS

UNIT 1   Patterns for the ii—V⁷—I Progression[1]

Transpose to all major keys. Play with Audio Track 25 on the Companion Website, www.routledge.com/cw/terefenko2e.

UNIT 2   Patterns for the ii∅—V⁷—i Progression[2]

Transpose to all minor keys. Play with Audio Track 26 on the Companion Website, www.routledge.com/cw/terefenko2e.

UNIT 3   Patterns for the III⁷—VI⁷—II⁷—V⁷ Progression

Transpose to all keys.

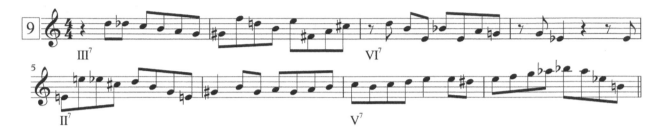

FUNDAMENTALS TO MASTERY

UNIT 4   Patterns for Blues Progressions

Basic Blues³

Exercise 4.1.1 **Ascending arpeggiated patterns with four-part chords.** Transpose to two additional keys. Play with Audio Track 1 on the Companion Website, www.routledge.com/cw/terefenko2e.

Exercise 4.1.2 **Descending arpeggiated patterns with four-part chords.** Transpose to two additional keys. Play with Audio Track 1 on the Companion Website, www.routledge.com/cw/terefenko2e.

Exercise 4.1.3 **"Lester Young" scale.**[4] Transpose to two additional keys. Play with Audio Track 1 on the Companion Website, www.routledge.com/cw/terefenko2e.

Exercise 4.1.4 **Blues riffs.** Transpose to two additional keys. Play with Audio Track 1 on the Companion Website, www.routledge.com/cw/terefenko2e.

Exercise 4.1.5 **Blues riffs.** Transpose to two additional keys. Play with Audio Track 1 on the Companion Website, www.routledge.com/cw/terefenko2e.

Minor Blues[5]

Exercise 4.2.1 **Four-part chords in inversions.** Transpose to two additional keys. Play with Audio Track 3 on the Companion Website, www.routledge.com/cw/terefenko2e.

Exercise 4.2.2 **Four-part arpeggiated patterns.** Transpose to two additional keys. Play with Audio Track 3 on the Companion Website, www.routledge.com/cw/terefenko2e.

Exercise 4.2.3 **Blues scale patterns.** Transpose to two additional keys. Play with Audio Track 3 on the Companion Website, www.routledge.com/cw/terefenko2e.

Exercise 4.2.4 **Blues motives.** Transpose to two additional keys. Play with Audio Track 3 on the Companion Website, www.routledge.com/cw/terefenko2e.

Exercise 4.2.5 **Arpeggiated patterns.** Transpose to two additional keys. Play with Audio Track 3 on the Companion Website, www.routledge.com/cw/terefenko2e.

The "Billie's Bounce" Progression

Exercise 4.3.1 **Inverted four-part chords.** Transpose to two additional keys. Play with Audio Track 27 on the Companion Website, www.routledge.com/cw/terefenko2e.

Exercise 4.3.2 **Five-part chords and bebop patterns.** Transpose to two additional keys. Play with Audio Track 27 on the Companion Website, www.routledge.com/cw/terefenko2e.

Exercise 4.3.3 **Bebop scales in different configurations.** Transpose to two additional keys. Play with Audio Track 27 on the Companion Website, www.routledge.com/cw/terefenko2e.

Exercise 4.3.4 **Various bebop patterns.** Transpose to two additional keys. Play with Audio Track 27 on the Companion Website, www.routledge.com/cw/terefenko2e.

Exercise 4.3.5 **Chromatic passing notes.** Transpose to two additional keys. Play with Audio Track 27 on the Companion Website, www.routledge.com/cw/terefenko2e.

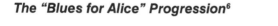

The "Blues for Alice" Progression[6]

Exercise 4.4.1 **Inverted four- and five-part chords.** Transpose to two additional keys. Play with Audio Track 28 on the Companion Website, www.routledge.com/cw/terefenko2e.

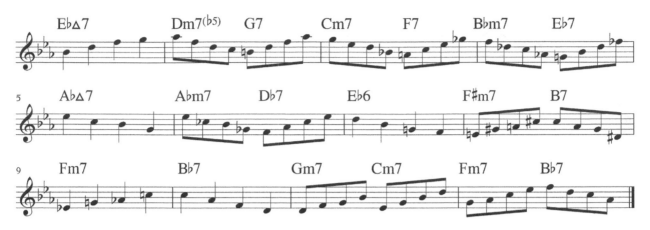

Exercise 4.4.2 Rootless five-part chords in inversions. Transpose to two additional keys. Play with Audio Track 28 on the Companion Website, www.routledge.com/cw/terefenko2e.

Exercise 4.4.3 Bebop patterns. Play with Audio Track 28 on the Companion Website, www.routledge.com/cw/terefenko2e.

Exercise 4.4.4 Bebop patterns. Transpose to two additional keys. Play with Audio Track 28 on the Companion Website, www.routledge.com/cw/terefenko2e.

Exercise 4.4.5 **Chromaticized bebop patterns.** Transpose to two additional keys. Play with Audio Track 28 on the Companion Website, www.routledge.com/cw/terefenko2e.

The "Dance of the Infidels" Progression[7]

Exercise 4.5.1 **Rootless five-part chords in inversions.** Transpose to two additional keys. Play with Audio Track 29 on the Companion Website, www.routledge.com/cw/terefenko2e.

Exercise 4.5.2 **Bebop patterns.** Transpose to two additional keys. Play with Audio Track 29 on the Companion Website, www.routledge.com/cw/terefenko2e.

Exercise 4.5.3 Bebop scales in rotations. Transpose to two additional keys. Play with Audio Track 29 on the Companion Website, www.routledge.com/cw/terefenko2e.

Exercise 4.5.4 Bebop patterns. Transpose to two additional keys. Play with Audio Track 29 on the Companion Website, www.routledge.com/cw/terefenko2e.

Exercise 4.5.5 Bebop patterns. Transpose to two additional keys. Play with Audio Track 29 on the Companion Website, www.routledge.com/cw/terefenko2e.

UNIT 5   The "Confirmation" Progression[8]

Exercise 5.1 First inversion four-part chords. Transpose to two additional keys. Play with Audio Tracks 30–32 on the Companion Website, www.routledge.com/cw/terefenko2e.

Exercise 5.2 Third inversion four-part chords. Transpose to two additional keys. Play with Audio Tracks 30–32 on the Companion Website, www.routledge.com/cw/terefenko2e.

Exercise 5.3 **Rootless five-part chords in inversions.** Transpose to two additional keys. Play with Audio Tracks 30–32 on the Companion Website, www.routledge.com/cw/terefenko2e.

Exercise 5.4 Arpeggiated patterns. Transpose to two additional keys. Play with Audio Tracks 30–32 on the Companion Website, www.routledge.com/cw/terefenko2e.

Exercise 5.5 **"Lester Young" scale.** Transpose to two additional keys. Play with Audio Tracks 30–32 on the Companion Website, www.routledge.com/cw/terefenko2e.

UNIT 6   The Rhythm Changes Progression[9]

Exercise 6.1 **Bebop scales.** Transpose to two additional keys. Play with Audio Tracks 33–35 on the Companion Website, www.routledge.com/cw/terefenko2e.

Exercise 6.2 **Rootless five-part chords in inversions.** Transpose to two additional keys. Play with Audio Tracks 33–35 on the Companion Website, www.routledge.com/cw/terefenko2e.

Exercise 6.3 **Rootless five-part chords in inversions.** Transpose to two additional keys. Play with Audio Tracks 33–35 on the Companion Website, www.routledge.com/cw/terefenko2e.

Exercise 6.4 Bebop scales and diminished chords. Transpose to two additional keys. Play with Audio Tracks 33–35 on the Companion Website, www.routledge.com/cw/terefenko2e.

Exercise 6.5 Bebop patterns. Transpose to two additional keys. Play with Audio Tracks 33–35 on the Companion Website, www.routledge.com/cw/terefenko2e.

MASTERY TO EXCELLENCE

UNIT 7   Modal Improvisation: Diatonic Modal Scales[10]

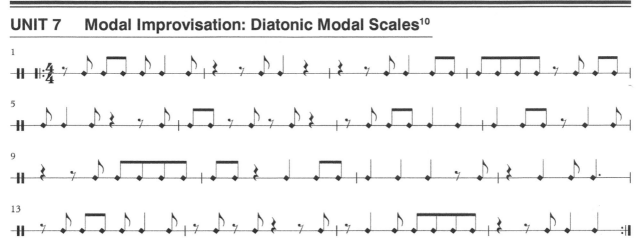

Exercise 7.1 Based on the given rhythmic phrase, improvise a solo using notes exclusively from D Ionian. Use Audio Track 5 on the Companion Website, www.routledge.com/cw/terefenko2e, for practicing modal improvisation with Ionian modes in 12 keys.

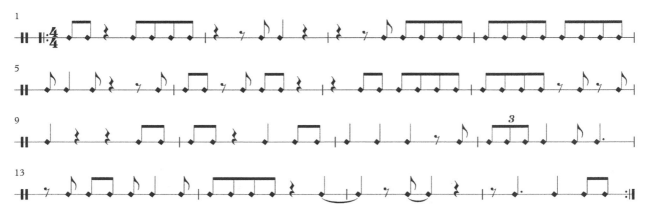

Exercise 7.2 Based on the given rhythmic phrase, improvise a solo using notes exclusively from E♭ Dorian. Use Audio Track 8 on the Companion Website, www.routledge.com/cw/terefenko2e, for practicing modal improvisation with Dorian modes in 12 keys.

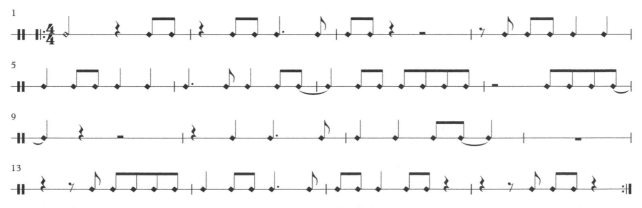

Exercise 7.3 Based on the given rhythmic phrase, improvise a solo using notes exclusively from G Phrygian. Use Audio Track 10 on the Companion Website, www.routledge.com/cw/terefenko2e, for practicing modal improvisation with Phrygian modes in 12 keys.

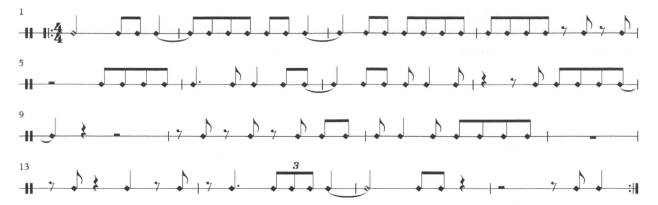

Exercise 7.4 Based on the given rhythmic phrase, improvise a solo using notes exclusively from A Lydian. Use Audio Track 6 on the Companion Website, www.routledge.com/cw/terefenko2e, for practicing modal improvisation with Lydian modes in 12 keys.

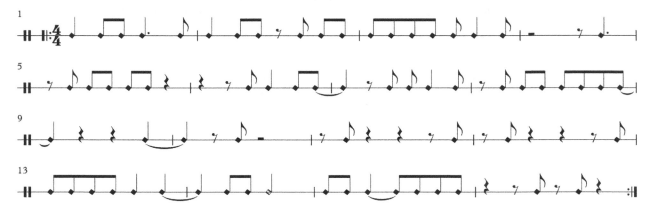

Exercise 7.5 Based on the given rhythmic phrase, improvise a solo using notes exclusively from B Mixolydian. Use Audio Track 7 on the Companion Website, www.routledge.com/cw/terefenko2e, for practicing modal improvisation with Mixolydian modes in 12 keys.

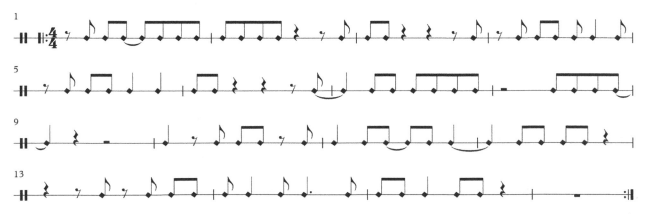

Exercise 7.6 Based on the given rhythmic phrase, improvise a solo using notes exclusively from B♭ Aeolian. Use Audio Track 9 on the Companion Website, www.routledge.com/cw/terefenko2e, for practicing modal improvisation with Aeolian modes in 12 keys.

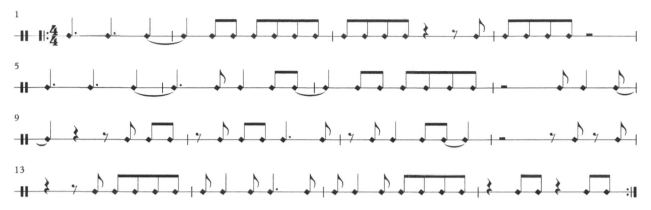

Exercise 7.7 Based on the given rhythmic phrase, improvise a solo using notes exclusively from Db Locrian. Use Audio Track 11 on the Companion Website, www.routledge.com/cw/terefenko2e, for practicing modal improvisation with Locrian modes in 12 keys.

UNIT 8   Modal Improvisation: Chromatic Modal Scales[11]

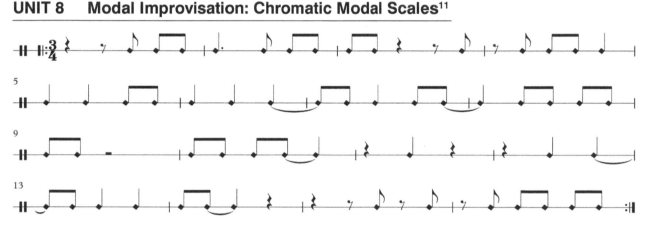

Exercise 8.1 Based on the given rhythmic phrase, improvise a solo using notes exclusively from F# Melodic Minor.

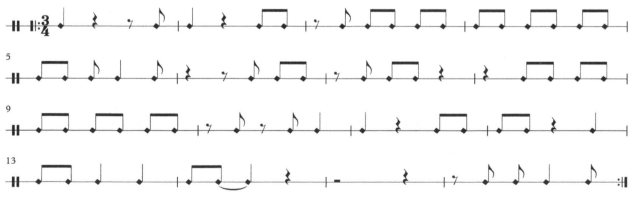

Exercise 8.2 Based on the given rhythmic phrase, improvise a solo using notes exclusively from E Dorian b2.

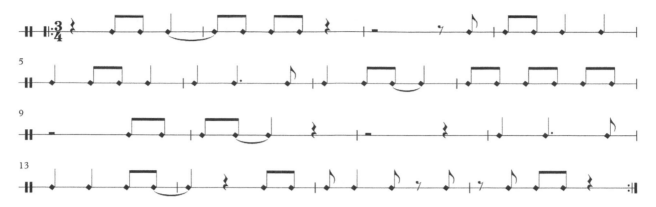

Exercise 8.3 Based on the given rhythmic phrase, improvise a solo using notes exclusively from A♭ Lydian Augmented.

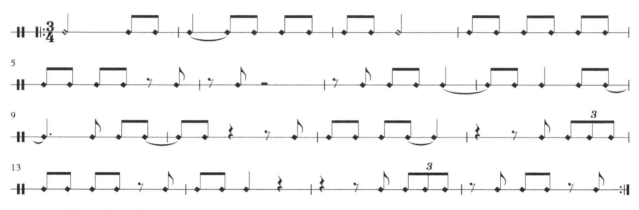

Exercise 8.4 Based on the given rhythmic phrase, improvise a solo using notes exclusively from C Mixolydian ♯11.

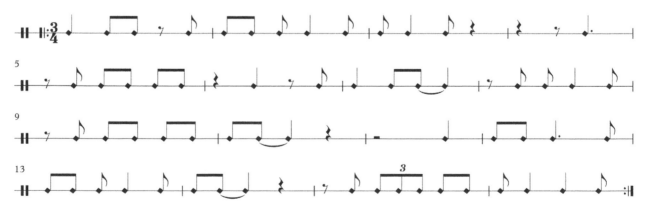

Exercise 8.5 Based on the given rhythmic phrase, improvise a solo using notes exclusively from D Mixolydian ♭13.

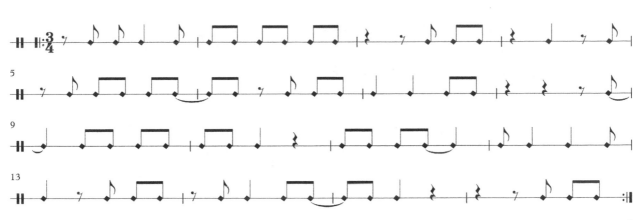

Exercise 8.6 Based on the given rhythmic phrase, improvise a solo using notes exclusively from C♯ Locrian ♮2.

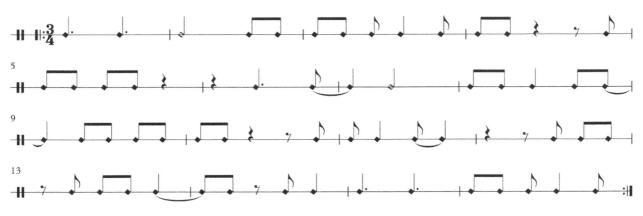

Exercise 8.7 Based on the given rhythmic phrase, improvise a solo using notes exclusively from A Altered.

NOTES

1. For the discussion of the ii—V⁷—I progression, consult Chapter 6 of *Jazz Theory—From Basic to Advanced Study*.
2. For the discussion of the iiᵒ—V⁷—i progression, consult Chapter 6 of *Jazz Theory—From Basic to Advanced Study*.
3. For the discussion of the blues, consult Chapter 9 of *Jazz Theory—From Basic to Advanced Study*.
4. The "Lester Young" scale is a major pentatonic with an added flatted third (blue note).
5. Consult Chapter 9 of *Jazz Theory—From Basic to Advanced Study*.
6. Consult Chapter 15 of *Jazz Theory—From Basic to Advanced Study*.
7. Consult Chapter 15 of *Jazz Theory—From Basic to Advanced Study*.
8. Consult Chapter 16 of *Jazz Theory—From Basic to Advanced Study*.
9. Consult Chapter 17 of *Jazz Theory—From Basic to Advanced Study*.
10. Consult Chapter 7 of *Jazz Theory—From Basic to Advanced Study*.
11. Consult Chapter 7 of *Jazz Theory—From Basic to Advanced Study*.